PORTUGUESE WOMEN IN TORONTO

Gender, Immigration, and Nationalism

Portuguese Women in Toronto

Gender, Immigration, and Nationalism

WENONA GILES

UNIVERSITY OF TORONTO PRESS
Toronto Buffalo London

© University of Toronto Press 2012
Toronto Buffalo London
www.utppublishing.com

ISBN 978-0-8020-3580-6 (cloth)
ISBN 978-1-4426-1495-6 (paper)

National Library of Canada Cataloguing in Publication Data

Giles, Wenona, 1949–
Portuguese women in Toronto : gender, immigration, and nationalism

Includes bibliographical references and index.
ISBN 978-0-8020-3580-6 (bound).   ISBN 978-1-4426-1495-6 (pbk.)

1. Portuguese Canadian women – Ontario – Toronto – Social conditions.
2. Women immigrants – Canada – Social conditions.   3. Sex role – Ontario –
Toronto.   I. Title.

HV4013.C2G54 2002   305.48′86910713541   C2001-903745-7

This book has been published with the help of a grant from the Humanities
and Social Sciences Federation of Canada, using funds provided by the Social
Sciences and Humanities Research Council of Canada.

University of Toronto Press acknowledges the financial assistance to its publishing program of the Canada Council for the Arts and the Ontario Arts
Council.

University of Toronto Press acknowledges the financial support for its publishing activities of the Government of Canada through the Book Publishing
Industry Development Program (BPIDP).

To Peter and to Siobhan

Contents

Tables, Figures, and Maps

Tables

Figures

Maps

Appendix

Preface

This book has its origins in the historical research I began in 1980 on gender relations and political consciousness in rural Portugal in the aftermath of the 1974 Portuguese socialist revolution. My interest in migration resulted in anthropological fieldwork in the Portuguese community of migrant men and women workers in London, England, in 1982–4, and a dissertation that I completed in 1987. In London I began my exploration of the relationship between household and wage workplace relations and the interweaving of these with the politics of migration. I interviewed Portuguese women and men who were employed in the domestic service sector, in hotels, hospitals, and private homes, mainly as cleaners and waiters, and I returned with them on their journeys in the summer, to towns and villages in Portugal. I found what I called 'forms of resistance' by women to gender inequalities in their wage workplaces and in the often invisible politics that occur in their households on an everyday basis. I hypothesized that there is a relationship between women's devalued role as unpaid workers in their own households and political struggles in the community and the workplace. This is a theme that has been of continuing interest to me: the linkages between the politics and social relations of the household, wage workplace, and the larger community.

After I completed the London research, I began to think about a comparative study with Portuguese in Toronto, to which there had been a large immigration and where I live and work. Although I had begun to address issues of difference and identity in my earlier research, I now addressed ethnicity and race in depth in studies of two generations of Portuguese women. By the time I began the work in Toronto in the early 1990s, feminists had made inroads into the study of gender and migration issues. The 1976 publication of *Anthropological Quarterly* on women and migration was the first collection of its kind, and demonstrated how women are affected by colonialism, socialism, and capitalism. Up to that time modernization theorists had stressed emigration as a matter of individual choice, rather than as a household strategy in which women had intimate involvement. Research in the 1980s began to address in earnest the experiences of immigrant women. A publication by Annie Phizacklea (1983) and a special issue of the *International Migration Review* edited by Mirjana Morokvasic (1984) provided important critiques of the migration literature and drew disciplines other than anthropology into research on gender and migration.

The ways in which citizenship is linked to ethnic/racial, class, and gender divisions became an important area of research for me as I began my work in Toronto. At that time Pateman (1989) was arguing that women are social exiles caught in a contradictory situation in which they contribute in the productive sphere, but are excluded from citizenship, which men have the prerogative to define. Although she did not address herself to immigrant and refugee women, her arguments concerning 'citizenship' were pertinent to my thinking about migration and women's exclusion from the 'nation.' Research by Floya Anthias and Nira Yuval-Davis on citizenship, ethnicity, and gender demonstrated how women are implicated in state systems that define 'family' in such a way that policies affecting immigrant women are formulated on the basis of a false separation between the public and private domain. Anthias and Yuval-Davis argued that policies regarding marriage and family relations contribute to the determination of women's status as citizens in the public domain (Yuval-Davis 1991; Yuval-Davis and Anthias 1989). Stasiulis, Arat- Koc, and others began to excavate the complexities of gender, nationalism, multiculturalism, and citizenship in Canada, beginning in the late 1980s and early 1990s (Stasiulis 1987, 1999; Arat-Koc 1990; Stasiulis and Jhappan 1995; Bakan and Stasiulis 1997). In recent years, many other important works on immigrant women and on Portuguese women have been written.

Comparative work has always been important to me. In the mid-1990s, building on comparisons across generations of Portuguese in Toronto, I collaborated in quantitative and qualitative studies of Chinese, Portuguese, Canadian-born women of British background, and other ethnic groups in Toronto who were wage workers in both the formal and informal economy. This research combined with my interest in global forms of restructuring, ethnicity/race, class, and gender relations.

This is an era of continual and bitter nationalist conflicts throughout the world, many of which result in extreme violence. My recent work on nationalism in militarized war zones (Giles and Hyndman forthcoming) undoubtedly has influenced my analysis of ethnicity and multiculturalism in Canada. However, my work on migration has helped me to understand how nationalism is related to global forms of restructuring, class, and racialization, issues that are missing in much current research about nationalism.

There are many individuals who have inspired and supported me in various ways in this endeavour. Ilda Januario, Luis Aguiar, Nora Jung, Caralee Price, and Brenda Cranney carried out many of the interviews with Portuguese and non-Portuguese participants. The anonymous reviewers, as well as Ilda Januario, Meg Luxton, and Valerie Preston provided invaluable and detailed critiques of earlier versions of the manuscript; Jane Springer and Jim Zimmerman gave me excellent editorial assistance and advice; Derrick Eberts helped me find the right statistical material; Carolyn King was meticulous with the maps; Nicole Groten transcribed many hours of tapes; Kim Phillips helped with final editing details and Mary Newberry skilfully and quickly completed the index.

My understanding of migration was deepened by discussions and debates about ethnicity, nationalism, and gender with friends and colleagues: Malathi de Alwis, Cathy Blacklok, Cynthia Cockburn, Alison Crosby, Cynthia Enloe, Vee Farr, Asha Hans, Jennifer Hyndman, Doreen Indra, Danielle Juteau, Edith Klein, Maja Korac, Audrey Macklin, Andjelka Milic, Shahrzad Mojab, Mirjana Morokvasic-Müller, Valerie Preston, Penny Van Esterik, Sandra Whitworth, Nira Yuval-Davis, and other members of the Women in Conflict Zones Network scattered throughout the world, and in particular in Sri Lanka and the region of the former Yugoslavia. At a number of critical points in this project Ilda Januario, Manuela Marujo, Deirdre Meintel, and Carlos Teixeira generously offered research advice concerning the Portuguese migration to Canada. Students in my nationalism, ethnicity, and gender seminar in the Women's Studies Graduate Programme at York University have also kept me continually challenged and inspired.

During the development of this book I have been sustained by friendship and scholarly critique from many, including Chris Bovaird, George Brody, Barbara Cameron, Blanche Giles, Don Giles, Susanne Jeffrey, Edith Klein, Sara Klein, Meg Luxton, Patricia McDermott, Rebecca McEvenue, Shelagh McEvenue, Barbara McGregor, Deirdre Meintel,

Haideh Moghissi, Saeed Rahnema, Ester Reiter, and Gerda Wekerle. Peter Murphy and Siobhan Giles Murphy have been loving, steadfast, and supportive throughout; their wisdom and humour have been my mainstay.

The many Portuguese women and men who were interviewed in Toronto for this book were gracious in sharing their very personal stories. Their careful reflection on their lives – here and in Portugal – as we sat in their homes, workplaces, or cafes drinking coffee, were always intriguing and, as some said, 'Como uma novela' (like a story). I would like to thank these women and men for their kindness, hospitality, and openness. I hope that I have represented them in a way that they consider true. I have done my best.

Funding for this Toronto-based research project was provided through a Social Sciences and Humanities Research Council of Canada fellowship, as well as a Secretary of State Research Grant and a Major Research Grant for Faculty at York University. During the course of this project, I was also grateful to collaborate with Valerie Preston on two other projects on ethnicity, gender, and restructuring in the Toronto labour market that contributed in critical ways to my thinking on this project. These projects were funded by the Social Sciences and Humanities Research Council of Canada (Women and Work Strategic Grant) and the Secretary of State (Canadian Ethnic Studies).

PORTUGUESE WOMEN IN TORONTO

Gender, Immigration, and Nationalism

Chapter One

Introduction

Nationalism in Canada, expressed in the politics of multiculturalism and in labour-market-oriented immigration policies, creates gender, class, and ethnic divides. In the process, many immigrant women and their descendants are defined differently from men in terms of their access to the rights and resources of the state. Nationalist projects, in which ethnic groups collectively identify with two (or more) nation-states, may appear to be strategically advantageous in an era of global restructuring, when downsizing and job losses have occurred in the sectors in which many immigrants are employed. In fact, nationalist projects are highly individualistic strategies which are limited in their provision of advantages to immigrants and their descendants, who cannot easily take on the identity of a dominant Anglo-European group. This kind of choice simply is not open (whether or not it is desirable) to most immigrants, contrary to recent arguments that we should all identify as 'ethnic Canadians' (Howard-Hassman 1999).[1] As Bottomley points out: 'The ability to choose or to challenge an identity ... is a measure of available spheres of freedom ... Ironically, one of the most potent threats to that degree of freedom comes from the delineation of collective identities' (Bottomley 1997:44).

This book examines the case of the Portuguese, analysing the creation and circumscription of Portuguese and Canadian collective nationalistic identities, whereby immigrants and their descendants, positioned as 'the other,' are limited in the extent to which they can choose or challenge an identity that would allow them equitable access to resources and rights. However, like many migrants, the Portuguese came to Canada to seek a better life:

[They] were very ambitious and wanted to expand and give their children an opportunity. What better place than in Canada or America? (Eunice, second-generation, accounting officer in bank, Azores)[2]

Portuguese migration around the world has continued for centuries, shaping the way Portuguese men and women define themselves at home and abroad. Emigration is described as 'Portugal's most constant modern historical phenomenon' (Baganha 1998:203); Canada is a country built upon immigration.

This book compares the household and working lives of Portuguese immigrant women with those of their daughters, some of whom were young immigrants themselves. The experiences of these women are relatively unknown and certainly underanalysed. Their lives offer challenging and revealing insights into the way Canada's immigration and multicultural policies operate to transform a highly heterogeneous group into the homogeneous category of 'immigrant.' I examine how this emphasis on ethnic identity conceals many other aspects of the lives of immigrants, most importantly, their contributions as workers in the Canadian labour market, in which immigrant women are often hidden or overlooked.

Migrations from the Portuguese mainland to Canada originated from four principal areas in the northerly regions of Portugal: Minho, Tras-os-Montes, Beira Alta, and Beira Baixa (Teixeira and Lavigne 1992). These immigrants had been employed principally as wage labourers in Portugal. Most of the Portuguese in Canada originate from the islands of the Azores, in particular the island of São Miguel, from rural backgrounds, and are considered relatively unskilled (Teixeira and Lavigne 1992). The move to Canada for this group meant a transition to an industrialized urban society.

Emigration from the Azores islands has tended to be to North America rather than to mainland Portugal or Europe, with some internal migration to jobs at the American military base on the island of Terceira. During the period from 1960 to 1975, the Azorean archipelago district of the capital city of São Miguel, Ponta Delgada, contributed almost 80 per cent of the total Azorean emigration to Canada (Higgs 1982:3). Because travel between the Azores and the Portuguese mainland has involved principally those (mostly men) who sought higher education or were completing military service on the mainland (Anderson and Higgs 1976:21–2), Portuguese immigrants from the mainland and the Azores often meet as a group for the first time in Canada.

The research for this book took place between 1989 and 1992 in Toronto, the Canadian city with the largest number of Portuguese immigrants (Nunes 1998:i). Sixty-one qualitative interviews were conducted with 20 first-generation Portuguese women, 17 second-generation women, 4 first-generation men, 4 second-generation men, and 16 Portuguese community workers in the Greater Toronto Area.[3] On Map 1.1, which indicates the settlement location of Portuguese in Toronto, I have noted the sites of most of the Portuguese households and the locations of the offices of Portuguese community workers who were part of this study.

For the purposes of this research, first-generation women are defined as those who came to Canada at age 15 or older, were unable to speak English fluently, and entered the workforce upon arrival. Second generation are those, born either in Portugal or in Canada, who attended school in Canada. This latter group has not faced the same English language fluency problems as the first-generation women. Thus, entry into wage labour upon arrival as well as access to the Canadian educational system demarcate the boundary dividing these women into two generations in my research. Portuguese migration, similar to other migrations to Canada, is primarily a labour migration, and thus the paid work–generational distinction that I employ is not an arbitrary one. Although child labour does exist in Canada, children cannot legally leave school until they are 15 years old, thus placing some age limitation on their employment. As well, education in Canada is a form of socialization that affects people's life trajectories (as this book demonstrates through various case histories).[4]

The reported number of Portuguese in Canada varies depending upon statistical sources and whether one defines Portuguese by their immigration status or their ethnic origin. The Portuguese Emigration Bureau maintains that between 1950 and 1988, 1,375,000 emigrants departed legally (i.e., not in a clandestine way)[5] from Portugal, and that five countries (France, Brazil, United States, Germany, and Canada, in order of importance) accepted 82 per cent of this total number of emigrants. The Bureau estimates that Canada received 138,000 Portuguese over this period of 38 years, representing 10 per cent of the total exodus (Baganha 1998:192–3) (see Map 1.2). In 1991 the Canadian census counted nearly twice as many people who defined their ethnic origin as Portuguese, at 246,890, with 176,300 in Ontario alone (based on responses by those who defined their ethnicity as solely Portuguese) (Citizenship and Immigration 1996; Teixeira 1995:74). To further

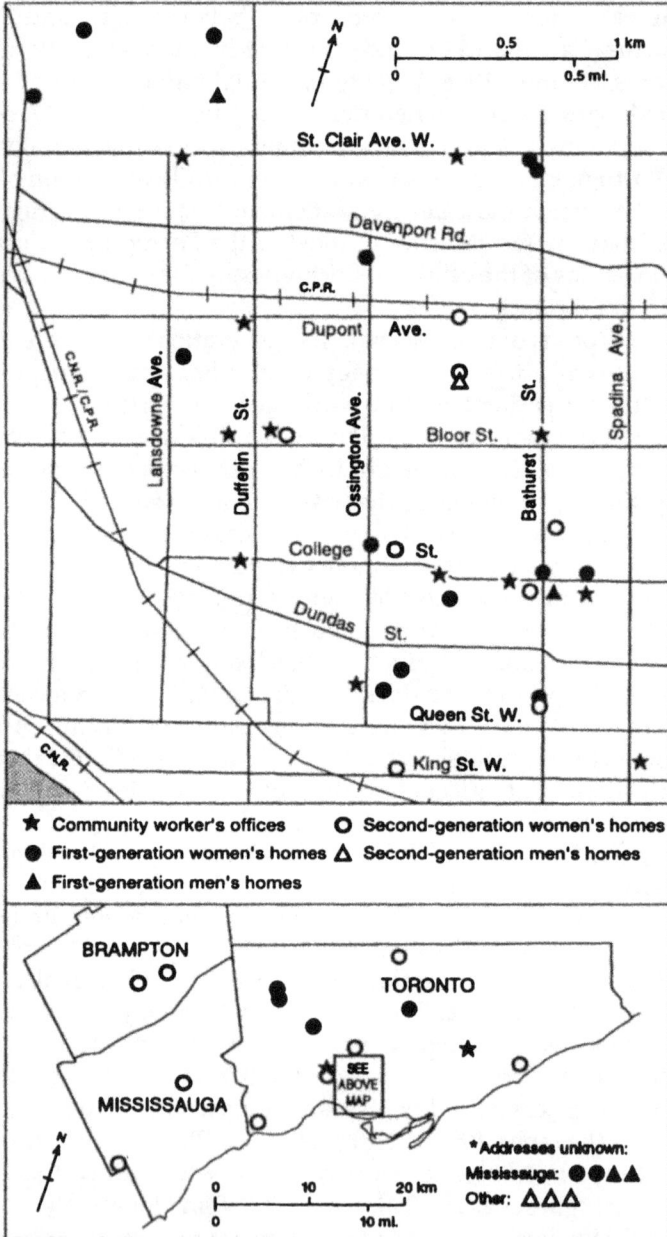

Map 1.1 Home/Office Locations of Those Interviewed in Toronto, Brampton, and Mississauga

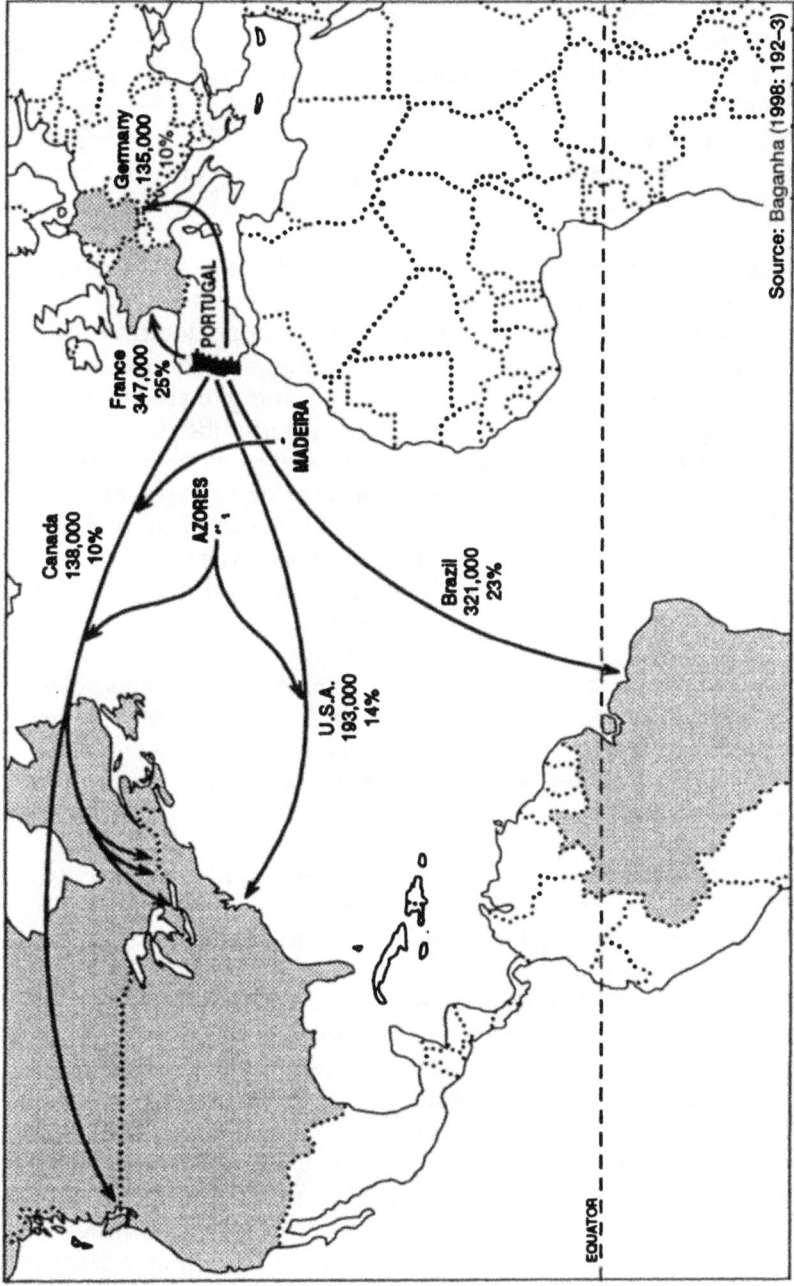

Map 1.2 Legal Portuguese Emigration to Principal Destinations, 1950–88

Germany
135,000
10%

France
347,000
25%

PORTUGAL

MADEIRA

AZORES

Canada
138,000
10%

U.S.A.
193,000
14%

Brazil
321,000
23%

EQUATOR

Source: Baganha (1998: 192–3)

complicate matters, in 1993 the Portuguese Consulate in Toronto estimated the numbers of Portuguese in Canada (of several generations) to be approximately 500,000, with 385,000 in Ontario (Teixeira and Lavigne 1992:4; Teixeira 1995:74). Contributing to the underestimation in official figures is the reluctance of many Portuguese to participate in the Canadian census because their allegiance lies elsewhere, they are illiterate, or they are clandestine immigrants and fear discovery by Canadian authorities.

At the time this research was carried out, Portuguese first-generation women worked in a variety of industries, but the majority were located in manufacturing and other services, which include domestic service work (Statistics Canada 1991). They were among the groups of immigrant workers most affected by the restructuring in manufacturing in the 1980s and 1990s. The backgrounds and opportunities for these first-generation women in Canada translated into average earnings of $17,000. Many of these women have worked at two or more types of jobs simultaneously in an effort to make ends meet and to counteract the harsh effects of economic restructuring on their lives (see Figure 4.1). Many are frustrated that the long hours of work leave little time for the responsibilities and pleasures of family life:

> Sometimes I came at 11:00, 11:30 [P.M.] for almost 11 years. So I saw my kids in that time, when they came home from school, just a little bit, from 4:00 until 5:00 in the evening ... just to prepare the dinner, put it on the table and go ... and then my husband came home. (Maria, cleaner, first generation, Azores)

Most first-generation women who live in Toronto are married; a small number are separated, but most do not live alone. In general, immigrants from Portugal (aged 15 to 64) are less likely to be single parents or to live in common-law relationships, and more likely to live with members of their immediate or extended family, than are members of other immigrant groups or Canadian-born. Portuguese men and women also are more likely to be living with a husband or wife, and Portuguese immigrant women have, on average, slightly more children (1.9 children) than other immigrant women (1.8 children) and Canadian-born women (1.6 children) (Citizenship and Immigration 1996:8). At the time they were interviewed in Toronto these women were between 32 and 59 years of age. Most had between three and seven years of formal education. The majority of the women were not able to return to school in Canada or to take advantage of language classes. Twenty per cent of the Portuguese living in Canada cannot converse in English or French (Citizenship and Immigration 1996:4). The effects of not being able to speak English were deeply felt by some of the women interviewed, who expressed frustration at not being able to defend themselves at work and in union meetings, thus raising the issue of what citizenship and democracy actually mean in the absence of the ability to communicate. Many Portuguese immigrant women did their best to acquire English-speaking skills by 'learning on the job.' Not being able to speak English has a spill-over effect to the second-generation Portuguese, some of whom described their resentment as young children when they were forced to become financial and bureaucratic translators and advisers to their parents, who could not speak English. However, many daughters also expressed a profound respect for their immigrant mothers:

> My mother has always worked, [and] I think from my perspective it showed me that she was capable of standing on her own two feet, being independent, as an individual. That always taught me to strive to be the same ... if anything it encouraged me to be more than just someone's daughter – or someone's wife – or someone's mother. (Eunice, second-generation, accounting officer in bank, Azores)

Second-generation Portuguese women work in a number of industries, but, from 1981 to 1996, the retail trade consistently was the most important employer of this group of women, followed by accommodation and food services, health and social services, and other services (Statistics Canada 1981, 1986, 1991, 1996) (see Table 4.1). The majority of the second-generation women interviewed in Toronto had parents who came from the Azores. Four of the women were born in Canada and the rest in the Azores and Portuguese mainland. At the time they were interviewed, these women ranged in age from 22 to 39 years. They earned average incomes of $27,000. More than half were either married or in common-law relationships. Not only had most of the second-generation women finished high school, but 76 per cent had attended some college or university, and more than half (53 per cent) of those who began a college or university degree had completed it (see Figure 5.1). These data challenge us to examine more closely the implications of gender on high school and university completion rates, particularly in light of a 1993 study that estimated that over 40 per cent of Portuguese high school students were at risk of dropping out (Toronto Board of Education 1993). In the study, the children of first-generation Portuguese parents were described as the second most likely immigrant group in Toronto to drop out of high school. My data indicate that Portuguese young women may be more successful than young men at academic achievement and completion of high school and post-secondary education, even though this may mean returning to finish their studies after an absence. One of the implications of the Toronto Board of Education study and other studies is that Portuguese parents are at least partly to blame for their children's curtailment of schooling. However, I found that many Portuguese parents have tried hard to keep their children in school, but that the school system often has thwarted their efforts. Nunes's study of the Portuguese in Canada points to a complex array of factors relating to the education of Portuguese youth that includes extreme pressure from some parents for their children to succeed academically, while others, for financial reasons, are discouraging. In addition, 'streaming,' racist stereotyping, and peer pressure are factors which contribute to the difficulty confronted by Portuguese in accessing education (1998:26–7, 1999; Aguiar 1994).

Many first-generation women who work in the cleaning industry and in factories have been actively involved in workplace and union politics, and take a critical view of their working conditions. One woman cleaner said that:

> [c]leaners are seen as someone without value, but they have more responsibility than the average person. We are treated like animals. Many women have left because they just can't take it. Of course they are replaced by new ones. These new ones are fired before they get into the union. (Amelia, office cleaner, first-generation, Azores)

However, the gender politics of these women are often more conservative than their labour politics. They express a predominant interest in preserving and protecting traditional gender roles in their households. In so doing, they sometimes clash with their daughters, who struggle for more egalitarian relations for their mothers and for themselves with husbands, fathers, brothers, and partners.

> My father initially felt threatened that she [my mother] was making it on her own two feet and quite capable of doing so. I think my father still harbours the same mentality that perhaps, he would be much more able to

control her, if she was at home and she was more dependent on him.
(Eunice, second-generation, accounting officer in bank, Azores)

Household gender relations have led to friction that has resulted in young women running away from home or moving out in order to attend university or live more independently. However, unlike their mothers, second-generation women are less politically active in the wage workplace. The majority of these women are located in non-unionized, female-dominated occupational sectors.

Subjects for this research were located with the assistance of community workers as well as through personal contacts. Every effort was made to ensure that the sample of women was as representative as possible of the community at large. Census material was reviewed carefully, and women were then chosen as subjects based on their occupational group and their regional origins (from the Portuguese islands or mainland). A detailed, open-ended questionnaire as well as a household survey were administered in Portuguese to first-generation women and men, and in English to second-generation women and men. The majority of the first-generation women whom we interviewed arrived between 1969 and 1975 from the Azores; others were from the mainland of Portugal (mainly Lisbon and the north), the island of Madeira, and Brazil.[6]

The process of analysing the gender relations of Portuguese immigrants in the context of Canadian immigration and multicultural practices encompasses several themes. The first of these is a critique of essentialist frameworks or discursive practices that construct a depoliticized notion of a homogeneous group of Portuguese immigrants in ways that mesh class, gender, and other characteristics around which people mobilize. This perspective is reflected in Grace Anderson's classic book on the Portuguese in Toronto, which describes them as an 'institutionally complete' ethnic group (1974:170). The extensive 'networks of [Portuguese] contact' that she writes about form the basis upon which she draws her conclusions about Portuguese immigration to Toronto in the early 1970s. However, Anderson provides little information about the lives of Portuguese women. The equation of supportive networking with so-called 'institutional completeness' is problematic, and arises out of a multiculturalist framework developed in Canada during the period when she did her research. My research indicates that Portuguese networks are complex, insofar as they are characterized not only by gender and class relations, but also by origin (e.g.,

Portuguese from the mainland or the Azores). Thus, the various groups of Portuguese in Toronto make greater or lesser use of networks or are involved in quite separate and different networks. This complexity challenges the possibility that there is either a homogeneous Portuguese network in Toronto or, indeed, an 'institutionally complete' Portuguese community based upon such a network. This is not to say that Portuguese have not been of assistance to one another in many ways, including finding jobs, housing, and schools for their children. However, these kinds of assistance are much removed from the tightly knit and self-sufficient group defined as 'institutionally complete.' Referring to a related concept of 'the ethnic enclave,' Estellie Smith describes how *unhelpful* a so-called ethnic community in the United States can be. In the words of one of her informants:

> Sure! They have people who speak Portuguese in the market, but sometimes their Portuguese is harder to understand than their English, and they look at you funny and you got to pretend you don't see they're laughing at your greenhorn ways. (Smith 1980:86)

The new immigrants' problems with shopping, the setup of an apartment or house in Canada, understanding transportation systems, communicating with schools and teachers – the everyday life of a housewife – have not necessarily been aided by an 'ethnic enclave.'

Government policies that define immigrants in this way deny the reality of the many gender, race, class, regional origin, generational, age, and other differences that exist for an immigrant group such as the Portuguese, thereby failing to recognize and address their diverse needs. Instead, definitions based on homogeneous notions of ethnic identity – such as 'Portuguese' – have become the basis for the distribution of state resources. Thus, although Canadian immigration and multicultural state policies may support those Portuguese who define themselves as such, there has been less enthusiasm about recognizing and addressing the needs of Portuguese women as immigrant *workers* who are part of a restructuring industrial workforce. These women have been defined traditionally as dependants of men, and not as members of the Canadian labour force. In fact, exclusionary immigration policies and practices have existed historically in Canada that either deny entry to immigrants (i.e., depending on origin, class, gender, or 'family' membership), or place restrictive definitions on some immigrants (i.e., women as dependants of men), while delivering a multiculturalist discourse of pluralistic acceptance. Canadian government multiculturalist policies have artificially defined a Portuguese community, creating boundaries that have more often served the interests of the Canadian state than Portuguese immigrants in Toronto.

A second theme of this book concerns the ways in which global political and economic inequities have affected Portuguese women's citizenship. Access to education, skills, and language training have played a major role in determining the types of employment opportunities open to Portuguese women and thus also to the possibilities for their participation in other aspects of life in Canada. In 1989, Zolberg wrote that 'No corner of the globe is now left that has not been restructured by market forces, uprooting the last remnants of subsistence economies and propelling ever growing numbers to search for work' (1989:404). He argued that, although most migration will continue to be internal to a country, those in poorer regions of the world undoubtedly will strive to migrate to wealthier regions. In their recent book on domestic workers in Canada, Bakan and Stasiulis point to the importance of international migration to sending countries, insofar as 'labour is currently the second most important "primary commodity" traded globally, the first being oil' (1997:30). They argue that the implications of global trade for citizenship practices have been under-analysed, and they and Calliste contend that 'entry into Canada for foreign domestic workers has always involved some trade-off between Third World and First World citizenship' (cited in Bakan and Stasiulis 1997:45). This trade-off has historically affected immigrant workers, such as Chinese, Italian, and Portuguese, who have worked in a variety of industrial sectors and who have experienced the discriminatory effects of Canada's nation-building goals and policies in similar racialized, gendered, and class-related ways (ibid.; Arat -Koc 1997; Iacovetta 1992; K. Anderson 1991).

A third theme arising out of the first two pertains to the relationship between the nationalisms of the two locales of the Portuguese diaspora: the Portuguese homeland state and the resettlement state of Canada. These nationalisms are intertwined with and mask economic restructuring and its consequences for immigrants and their descendants. On the one hand, the exclusionary politics of Canadian nationalism, expressed through a facade of pluralistic multiculturalism, limits access to Portuguese wishing to enter Canada; on the other hand, a Portuguese nationalism links emigrants with Portugal through a web of economic, political, and social relationships, and promises that is expressed in return migration and remittances to Portugal. Together, these nationalisms, which are *both* situated in historical forms of economic restructuring, contribute to definitions of home for Portuguese immigrants.

It is an at least partly illusory and often invisible sense of home that defines and/or identifies a people. This identity is linked to a group's gender politics, as well as the potential for, and the limitations to, its political action. Nationalism is usually associated with a discourse about the family or homes of the nation, women as 'mothers of the nation,' family values, and the role of women in ensuring that these values and morals are upheld. Women in particular stand to lose in this kind of nationalist discourse, as their dependency on men becomes either assumed or imposed. In this book I am proposing a methodology for thinking through the limitations of both Canadian and Portuguese nationalisms.

These three themes weave throughout the following chapters and are analysed more specifically in the concluding chapters. Chapter Two is a history of Portuguese migration to Canada and Canadian immigration policy. In it, I examine the concurrence of the arrival of large numbers of Portuguese to Canada in the mid to late 1960s to the early 1980s with the establishment of the Immigration Act of 1967 and the Federal Multiculturalism policy of 1971. At that time in Portugal, in the aftermath of the Portuguese Revolution of 1974, economic recession and high unemployment and the forced repatriation of 400,000 Portuguese from the former African colonies, along with 100,000 soldiers (Baganha 1998:202), contributed to the increased emigration of Portuguese men and women. The issue of Portuguese regionalism is raised as a challenge to ideas of a homogeneous Portuguese immigrant community. Examples of remittances by Portuguese to Portugal and return migration are explored as individualistic and limited strategies of resistance to the inequities of international migration. This chapter begins to redress the relative absence of Portuguese women in migration histories.

The book's case studies begin by focusing on the household, and then move out from there to the wage workplace and to other aspects of women's lives. Chapter Three explores the Portuguese household through the stories of four women – two of each generation – who express very different experiences of migration to Canada, related to class, education, regional origin, age, and other differences in their lives. Using a life history and comparative approach, this chapter discusses definitions of household and home, as well as the related issues of return migration and return orientation.

Chapter Four analyses the wage workplaces of Portuguese women through a case study of the working life of a Portuguese immigrant woman. Here again stereotypical definitions of 'the Portuguese woman' are challenged, as is the emphasis on ethnic identity rather than identity as a worker. The economics and politics of the household and wage workplace are addressed in this chapter as a way of challenging static notions of ethnic identity and raising questions about class identity. As well, the workplace politics and class consciousness of Portuguese immigrant women are explored through two cases of workplace resistance: a strike by cleaners and another by factory workers. Most of the Portuguese women who participated in these strikes were first-generation immigrants. Some comparisons are drawn here with the more liberal-based politics of second-generation women.

In the two chapters that follow, the book continues to rely on empirical material, but moves away from a life history approach to address more directly and theoretically issues of nationalism and multiculturalism. Chapter Five focuses on ethnicity and nationalism in Canada. Here I argue that we need to look beyond the promotion of cultural authenticity to broader-based solidarities in order to resist racial, ethnic, class, gender, and other inequities that immigrants and their descendants experience. The first part of the chapter addresses Portuguese ethnic identity. In the second part of the chapter, I take the specific case of education and examine the effects of multiculturalist education policies on three groups of women: first- and second-generation Portuguese women and Canadian anglophone working-class women.

The final chapter pursues the issue of the exclusiveness of multiculturalism, arguing that Canadian discourse and policies pertaining to immigration have persisted in creating boundaries between white persons of British anglophone backgrounds and others, such as the Portuguese in Canada. Prioritizing struggles for the recognition of ethnocultural identity over struggles for equal access to education, employment, and health resources is identified as a limited form of resistance that conforms to the ideology and practice of state multiculturalism in Canada. Finally, I point to alternative, feminist ways of analysing nationalist discourse and practice.

These themes form the framework of my critique of a Canadian nationalism and multiculturalism which encourages ethnic groups to identify with two (or more) nation-states. Multiculturalist policies lead to highly individualistic strategies which are limited in their utility for immigrants and their descendants, who find they cannot easily take on the identity of 'ethnic Canadian.'

Chapter Two

Where Have All the Women Gone?

Fragments about the lives of Portuguese immigrant women in Canada can be found in state archival material, census data, newspaper stories, and the scant references to their journeys and arrivals in histories of migrations to Canada. Their relative absence in historical records is related to the way in which both immigration and multicultural policy, and most researchers and writers, have defined them as dependants or wives of men. Over fifteen years ago, Estellie Smith explained why Portuguese Azorean women in the United States, like other immigrant women, have been invisible in studies of migration. She wrote that women's 'structural significance has been skewed; their processual importance ignored; and their roles as humans treated as limited, trivial and inconsequential' (Smith 1980:80). As feminists have searched for the women 'hidden from history' (Rowbotham: 1973), some have begun to explore the gender relations of migrations, including the Portuguese migration to Canada, mostly by interviewing women and men who have remembered and reconstructed the gendered experiences of their migration (see for example, Cole 1998; Giles 1993, 1997; Januário and Marujo 2000; Labelle et al. 1987; Noivo 1997).[1] Gendering the history of Portuguese migration to Canada involves more than simply adding or subtracting from data on men and women.

It is a challenge to find marginalized women's experiences described in written histories. As writers of gendered histories, we engage in a 'deconstruction' of historical records to locate invisible women and give life and voice to their stories. This undertaking involves challenging traditional paradigms of women as passive dependants or wives of active migrant men. Joan Scott points out that such feminist deconstruction does more than simply correct or supplement an incomplete historical record, it provides a critical understanding of how history produces knowledge about gender relations (1988:10). She argues that written histories, building on other histories that do not question normative notions of the masculine and feminine, distort the history of gender relations. Feminist historians engage in a disruption of the 'notion of fixity, to discover the nature of the debate or repression that leads to the appearance of timeless permanence in binary gender representation' (ibid. 43).

There are at least two related reasons for the general absence of women in migration histories. First, there is an assumption implicit in much migration research that the worlds of wage work and unpaid household work are separate and independent spheres, with women located in the household and men in wage work. When women are 'foregrounded' (Indra 1996) in the household as mothers, wives, and daughters, they disappear elsewhere as migrants, workers, and citizens. Second, immigration and multiculturalist policies, linked as they are to nationalism, define immigrant women in patriarchal ways, contributing to their invisibility in state policies and legislation and thus also in migration histories. In these discourses,[2] women are regarded as essential to the transference of ethnic and cultural traditions, including definitions of appropriate gender relations. States often administer and / or integrate the gendered practices of various ethnic groups when these serve the purposes of the state's policies. Thus, cloaked in cultural relativism, the state may support the retention of 'the old country' culture by downplaying the importance of women's contribution outside the household and promoting their role as wives and mothers.

In this chapter, I first explore the relationship between multiculturalism and immigration policy in Canada, and then, using the history of Portuguese migration to Canada, describe how these policies, have affected a particular immigrant group. Portuguese migration to Canada exemplifies the ways in which the multiculturalist discourse has been used to define an immigrant population and how that population has responded. The story of the migration of Portuguese to Toronto unfolds in a context of immigration and multicultural policies that have defined who may enter Canada and the circumstances of their entry and settlement. These policies, working together with national and international forms of economic restructuring, have contributed to worldwide migration, especially now that global restructuring has influenced the creation of a 'Fortress Europe,' and an emerging, but differently organized, 'Fortress North America.' In the case of Canada, the fortress is built by increasing harmonization of immigration and refugee policies with the United States; an economically driven association with Mexico that is politically ambiguous, since Canada receives refugees from that country; and a resistance to labour migration, except at the elite levels of multinational management, professional, and technical staff, and at the lowest echelons of the least desirable, highly controlled migrant labour jobs.

In this chapter, I argue that it is no coincidence that the most intense migration of Portuguese occurred between 1968 and 1977. Rather, it was the result of (1) the concern of Portuguese to enter before the full implementation of the increasingly stringent requirements of the Canadian Immigration Acts; (2) the establishment of the Federal Multicultural Policy in 1971; and (3) the formulation of the Portuguese Emigration Policy in 1976, in the aftermath of the 1974 socialist democratic revolution in Portugal and the end of the Portuguese colonial wars in Africa. Figure 2.1 shows the relationship between Portuguese migration to Canada since the 1960s and Canadian and Portuguese state policies.

Canadian Immigration and Multicultural Policies

The exclusivity of Canadian immigration policy is embedded in global economic and political relations that have defined some immigrant populations as welcome and others not. This is what Li (1988:135) describes as 'a cost or benefit associated with each origin in the capitalist labour market.' The cost or benefit of an immigrant is related to competing state interests that historically have been manifested in a demand for labour rather than political support for immigrants of a particular class, gender, or racial background. For example, business-class immigrants have been preferred to working-class immigrants, and refugees from the former Yugoslavia have been preferred to those from Rwanda. A global perspective on migration exposes the inequities of multiculturalism policies, by demonstrating the relationship between global economics and the maintenance of nation-state boundaries. Basch et al. point out that this approach challenges us to see beyond the confines of concepts such as 'nation, ethnic group and tribe that divide the world into autonomous, geographically rooted and culturally distinct units' (Basch et al. 1994:33). The reasons for the construction of these boundaries, and the ways in which the boundaries are used, once established, are revealing (ibid. 33). Immigrant women historically have had the most to lose, because, despite their apparent gender neutrality, Canadian immigration and multicultural policies are deeply

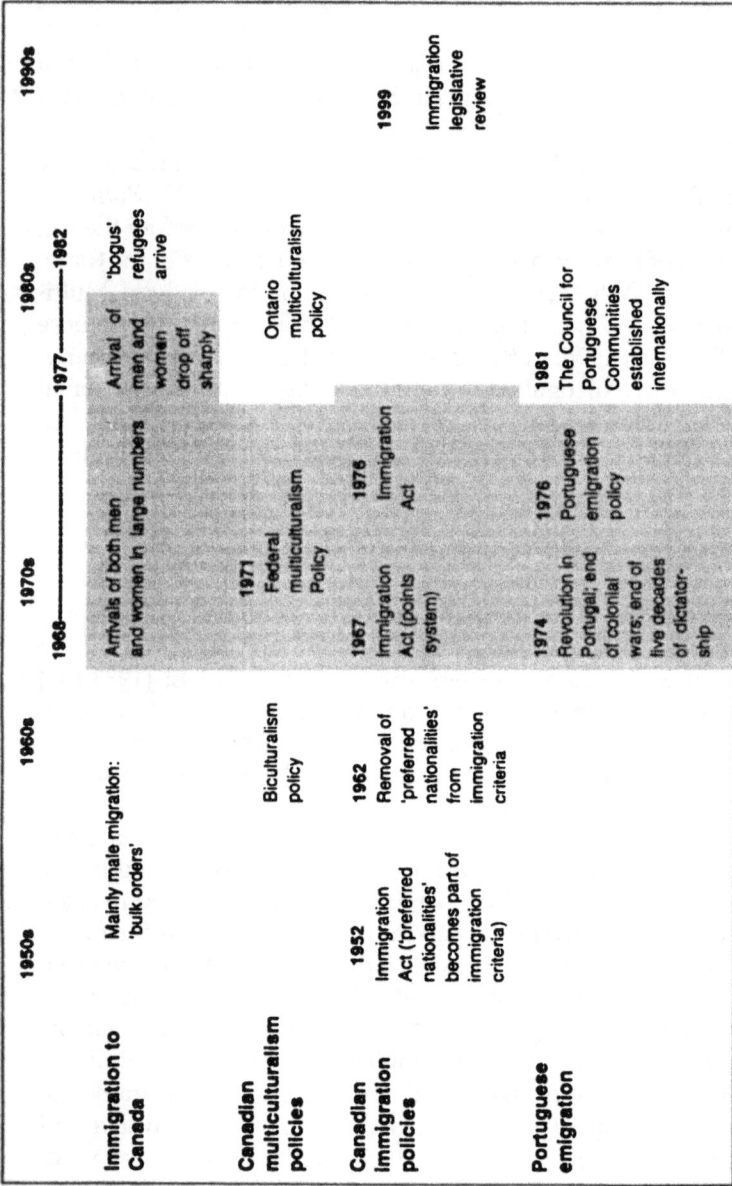

	1950s	1960s	1970s	1980s	1990s
Immigration to Canada	Mainly male migration: 'bulk orders'		Arrivals of both men and women in large numbers	Arrival of men and women drop off sharply / 'bogus' refugees arrive	
Canadian multiculturalism policies		Biculturalism policy	1971 Federal multiculturalism Policy	Ontario multiculturalism policy	
Canadian Immigration policies	1952 Immigration Act ('preferred nationalities' becomes part of immigration criteria)	1962 Removal of 'preferred nationalities' from immigration criteria	1967 Immigration Act (points system) / 1976 Immigration Act		1999 Immigration legislative review
Portuguese emigration			1974 Revolution in Portugal; end of colonial wars; end of five decades of dictatorship / 1976 Portuguese emigration policy	1981 The Council for Portuguese Communities established internationally	

Timeline markers: 1968 — 1977 — 1982

Note: The shaded area indicates a concurrence of events and policies in Portugal and in Canada that contributed to and affected the large labour migration of Portuguese men and women to Canada in the decade between the late 1960s and the late 1970s.

Figure 2.1. Portuguese Migration to Canada from the 1960s to the Present in Relationship to Immigration and Multiculturalism Policies in Canada and Portugal

gendered and have significantly shaped the experiences of Portuguese immigrant women in Canada, as the 1976 Immigration Act reveals: 'Canada's third Immigration Act of 1976 sets as its general purpose: immigration policy ... designed and administered ... to promote the domestic and international interests of Canada' (Immigration Act, Preamble, Section 3, 1976). The interpretation of this Act in subsequent regulations has confirmed the Canadian government's labour-market orientation and revealed its androcentric underpinnings. Sexist definitions of 'skill' and 'work' have delimited and defined immigrant women as dependants in subordinate positions. As well, heterosexist familial policies that historically have linked immigrant women's status to that of a male partner or father have contributed to the dependency of immigrant women on men.

As I (and others) have argued in a study of Canadian and Australian immigration policy, sexist definitions of work and skill in immigration policies are inappropriate and ignore major feminist critiques made over the last two decades (Fincher et al. 1994). The majority of women who enter Canada as immigrants and refugees enter as dependants rather than workers, even though they may be wage workers who intend to continue working. Their work, education history, and gender are regarded as not measuring up to the requirements demanded of independent immigrants. In fact, until 1974, married women were not allowed to enter Canada as principal immigrant applicants, regardless of their qualifications (Boyd 1975).

In recent times, a points system has been developed to evaluate immigrants. This system has undergone repeated amendment, with major changes in 1978 and 1985, that increased the weight given to the applicant's perceived ability to satisfy current labour market demands (Fincher et al. 1994). Proposed changes outlined in the Immigration Legislative Review document, *Not Just Numbers: A Canadian Framework for Future Immigration* (Immigration Legislative Review Advisory Group 1997),[3] further emphasized the need for skilled workers, while broadening the definition of 'family.' However, the extent to which sponsoring immigrants may be able to bring in family members depends increasingly on financial resources, since they are expected to pay a variety of fees, including an administrative fee, a newly proposed language training fee for each person entering the country, and a right of landing fee or 'head tax'(recently rescinded), a sum which amounted to more than two thousand dollars per person. As well, attempts have been made to deny Canadian citizenship to children born to non-citizens in Canada.[4] Policies proposed in *Not Just Numbers* concerning language skills and training fees affect the access of many women who have not had the same opportunities as men to benefit from language education in their home countries, or who are unable to pay the training fee. New restrictions on sponsoring family members if the sponsor has been on welfare during the preceding twelve months affect women in particular, as sponsors or as prospective immigrants (OCASI 1998:6–7). Immigrant groups have argued that these overall costs 'will create barriers to establishing a good financial basis to meet family reunification guidelines and prolong the separation of family members,' and that they have 'a disproportionate impact upon women and the poor given that worldwide they have lesser access to education' (OCASI 1998:4). As the National Action Committee on the Status of Women (NAC) points out, the Immigration Legislative Review report lacks not only a gender analysis in its recommendations, but 'fails to acknowledge and address existing bias and discrimination against women in the immigration and refugee systems' (Arat-Koc 1999b:18).[5]

Historically, the Canadian government has promoted its policies towards immigrants, as well as towards Quebec and Native peoples' aspirations for autonomy, under the rubric of multiculturalism. This policy, initially intended as a means of managing Canadian-born francophones, has evolved through its relationship with immigration policy to become a means of controlling immigrant groups.

The federal policy on multiculturalism was adopted in 1971 by the Liberal government of Pierre Trudeau at the very time Portuguese migration to Canada was at its peak (see Figure 2.1). Although this policy was 'conceived as a form of cultural – rather than structural – pluralism' (Dorais et al. 1994:386), it is aligned with Canada's economic and political policies. Canadian immigration and multicultural policies are economically and politically intertwined, and employ a common discourse in their goals of defining, managing, and controlling immigrant populations. However, defining immigrants in Canada in a multiculturalist way, as members of particular ethnic minority communities, entails a symbolic recognition that the nation-state comprises more than one ethnic group and a variety of cultural traditions that are 'complementary and reconcilable with each other' (Stasiulis and Yuval-Davis 1995:26; Yuval-Davis 1992).

Bottomley describes multiculturalism as 'encourag[ing] an openness to difference,' but also argues that this 'is limited by the presentation of multiculturalism within a political framework of pluralism, of parallel and homogeneous differences that serve to emphasise certain aspects of ethnicity and ignore others.' She describes ethnic and cultural purity as 'increasingly illusory,' and argues that we need instead to understand the ways in which 'ideas, beliefs and practices ... are being transformed and renegotiated in different contexts and reassembled in specific social fields' (1995a:16).

In negotiations between Canadian state policy-makers and immigrant groups, it is usually the male, conservative leadership of immigrant groups that interprets cultural difference within the community (Stasiulis and Yuval-Davis 1995:27). In this process, gender and class differences are masked, and ethnic differences are reified, contributing ultimately to racism. Definitions of these ethnic groups generally presume an internal cohesion among members of the so-defined groups, which leads to the separation of each group from the others. Gender, class, age, generation, and other differences diminish in importance as an overarching ethnic identity defines a specific immigrant group in opposition to non-immigrants and to other immigrants. Even the descendants of immigrants often are encompassed in these categories, generating a discourse that defines Portuguese in Canada as Portuguese Canadians, an identity that is neither Canadian nor Portuguese.

Multiculturalsm, in the absence of associations through which immigrants can express their opposition to the inequality and oppression they experience in their workplaces, households, schools, and neighbourhoods, has been described as 'a politics of resistance' to assimilation (Brah 1996:227, 230). The restructuring of Canadian and international economies plays a significant role in defining the 'contexts' and 'specific social fields' in which Portuguese immigrants and their descendants live and work. Multiculturalist discourse, appearing under a humanistic guise of cultural pluralism, historically has contributed to the invention/creation of communities that serve the purposes of industrial capitalist development in Canada.

Portuguese Migration to Canada

Canadian immigration policy and the multiculturalist politics that have underpinned it have been ambiguous at best and highly restrictive at worst towards the Portuguese. Although these intertwined policies treat them as such, the Portuguese are by no means a homogeneous group of immigrants. Differences of gender, class, and regional origin have all affected the experiences of Portuguese desiring to come to

Canada. Most Portuguese women have entered Canada under different circumstances from those of men, thus affecting gender relations both inside and outside the household. Women, because they generally have entered Canada as dependants of men, have been treated differently both by Canadian settlement policy and by employers. Class differences, which relate to levels of education and skill, work experience, economic resources, and geographical origins, also have implications for settlement in Canada, where immigration policy has increasingly favoured more highly skilled and educated immigrants. Portuguese immigrants to Canada range from the illiterate to the highly skilled and well-educated. Portuguese from the islands of the Azores and Madeira differ significantly from those from the mainland of Portugal in their economic, political, and cultural background. These differences have led to different attitudes towards settlement in Canada, as well as to dissension between regional groups that have settled here. The response of the Portuguese in Toronto to state multiculturalism has included a discourse that tends to downplay regional tensions within the population in an effort to create a united front (i.e., between those immigrants from the islands of the Azores and Madeira and those from the mainland). Canadian immigration policy and multiculturalism policies have interacted with this heterogeneous Portuguese immigrant population to produce a Portuguese-Canadian identity, itself stratified by class, gender, and regional differences.

The Early Years

The Portuguese began to engage seriously in international labour migration in the 1700s, attracted by the discovery of gold in Brazil at the end of the 1600s. Prior to this time, migration was tied mainly to colonizing missions begun in the sixteenth century in Brazil, North America, Asia, and Africa (Godinho 1971). However, it is likely that there has been Portuguese temporary migrant labour in Canada since the sixteenth century, when Portuguese fishers first came to Newfoundland, attracted by the abundance of cod and the availability of trade with other European colonizers (Abreu-Ferreira 1995–6:23). As far as we know, few Portuguese women came to Canada in these early days of migration and colonization, when Portugal, Britain, France, and Spain were contending for the best fishing grounds along the Newfoundland coast (Anderson and Higgs 1976:11). Most Portuguese came from the north of mainland Portugal. The town of Viana do Castelo, in particular, is described as possessing 'solid and consistent documentation of its early connection with Newfoundland' (Abreu-Ferreira 1995–6:18). On the east coast of Canada, Portuguese fishers were part of the development of the fishing industry (Anderson and Higgs 1976:9). There is also evidence that, in the early years of the nineteenth century, Portuguese men travelled as far inland as the MacKenzie River, and at least a few interacted with the native population.

Portuguese migration is also characterized by a regionalism that dates back to the fifteenth century, when the Algarve region of south Portugal sent immigrants to the newly occupied Atlantic islands of Madeira and the Azores, as well as to other Portuguese colonies, including the Cape Verde Islands, São Tomé, and the Congo. In the sixteenth century, emigrants began to travel from the northwest region of mainland Portugal to a variety of international destinations, and by the latter quarter of the seventeenth century a secondary migration began from the Azores and Madeira to North and South America (Chaney 1986:106). These patterns persisted to some extent into the twentieth century, with the majority of Portuguese in Canada coming from the Azores, and a substantial, but smaller number from the north of Portugal.

By the seventeenth century, the new labour migration (i.e., to places outside the colonies) of mainly male working-class and peasant populations began to overtake the importance of migrations associated with the Portuguese colonial state, and was described by social commentators at the time as beginning to seriously deplete the population. However, it was also recognized 'as an economic solution for the poorer classes of rural Portugal' (Faria and Macedo in Brettell 1986:75). From the early eighteenth century into the nineteenth century, issues such as the relationship between the increase in the salaries of manual workers and the out-migration of this class of worker led to restrictive emigration laws in Portugal (ibid. 76). Thus, clandestine emigration became a fact of life for Portuguese from the eighteenth century into the twentieth century. Demographic pressures on the land in some parts of Portugal, crop disease in the wine industry, protests against taxes on rural labour, increasing speculation, and expropriation of land by the wealthy classes, and avoidance of military service all contributed to the nineteenth century migrations. Brettell's detailed study of emigration from a parish in northern Portugal indicates that it was common in the eighteenth to twentieth centuries for young men and women to postpone their marriage for five years or more, until they were able to secure enough money from sources such as labour migration to sustain a new household. In other words, emigration was an essential fact of life 'in a region where opportunities for lucrative, salaried nonagricultural labour were limited' (Brettell 1986:114, 116–19).

The Post-war Years

Canadian immigration policy always implicitly, if not explicitly, has differentiated between prospective immigrants on the basis of ethnicity, and until 1951, reserved 'preferential treatment' for British and French subjects. Immigration policy was broadened at that time to include northwestern European countries, but not the Portuguese. As southern Europeans, they were ambiguously located somewhere between (but outside of) the preferred nationalities, and the group of non-traditional (non-European) immigrants. The 1952 Immigration Act continued the policy of 'preferred nationalities' and it was not until 1962 that the preferential treatment regulations were removed and replaced by an emphasis on education and skills. However, the new orientation still allowed Canada to discriminate on the basis of class, region, and gender, by choosing immigrants whose education and skill most closely matched those of a Eurocentric and male-oriented immigration policy.

The ethnic and racial discrimination inherent in definitions of labour force requirements have characterized official Canadian immigration policy and shaped migration flows. Portuguese male farmworkers followed the 'bulk orders' of mainly 'unskilled' male Italian workers in the period immediately following World War II (Iacovetta 1992:28), though in much smaller numbers, and were among those sought to work on the farms and railway lines across Canada.[6] In 1954, the Portuguese and Canadian governments collaborated to recruit men from the Portuguese mainland and the Azores to work in remote areas of Canada, on the railway lines, on farms, and as tradesworkers (Hawkins 1988:49–50; Anderson and Campbell Davis 1990). This practice of importing a highly exploitable labour force, juxtaposed to 'male, white and British skilled craft workers,' was a central feature of Canada's 'overtly racist immigration policies' (Stasiulis and Jhappan 1995:98) of the time and underwrote the development of its multicultural policy.

According to Hawkins (1988), these 'bulk orders' began in 1954 with 200 railway track workers, 700 agricultural workers for mixed farms, and up to 50 tradesworkers, all from the Azores. The following year, 900 farm labourers and 50 tradesworkers were selected from the Portuguese mainland. In 1956, a similar program selected workers from the Azores, and in 1957, 2,000 farm labourers (1,000 from the Azores and 1,000 from the mainland) as well as 50 tradesworkers[7] arrived in Canada. In 1957, 1,000 railway track workers from the Azores were recruited for the W.R.Welsh Company (Hawkins 1988:49–50).

The Conservatives, who were in power in Canada from 1957 to 1963, encouraged Portuguese immigration to Canada as a source of cheap labour. Portuguese immigrants from the Azores were regarded in the same way that southern Italians had been in earlier times. The Department of Citizenship and Immigration in a 1963 Departmental Report reflects on this migration:

> About this time (1957–58) serious doubts began to be felt in the Immigra-
> tion Branch about the Portuguese movement. The Portuguese Govern-
> ment was obviously making efforts to concentrate our recruiting activities
> in the Azores. At the same time there were increasing signs that the
> declining need for unskilled labourers in Canada would not continue to
> support the type of movements we had been accepting in Portugal. The
> several large movements of unskilled workers from the Azores showed
> signs of producing a disproportionate volume of sponsored immigrants
> (duplicating our experience in Italy). (Department of Citizenship and
> Immigration 1963)

Finally, the Conservative government put a halt to the 'bulk' orders of Portuguese male workers. At this time Portuguese began to apply from within Canada for landed status which, after a period of residency, would lead to citizenship.

The fear that sponsored immigrants would flood into Canada to join their relatives (i.e., unskilled workers who had arrived earlier), led to attempts to restrict this movement. In 1959 the Department of Citizen-ship and Immigration tried unsuccessfully to restrict the admissible class of relatives to the immediate family. A second effort began with the publication of the White Paper on Canadian Immigration Policy in 1966. This document stipulated that Canadian citizenship should be a necessary requirement for sponsoring relatives. This meant it would take years longer to bring sponsored immigrants to Canada. Finally, in 1967, the new Department of Manpower and Immigration announced an Immigration Act and immigration regulations that awarded points to independent applicants for specific entry criteria. In addition, admission criteria stipulated the separation of dependent from non-

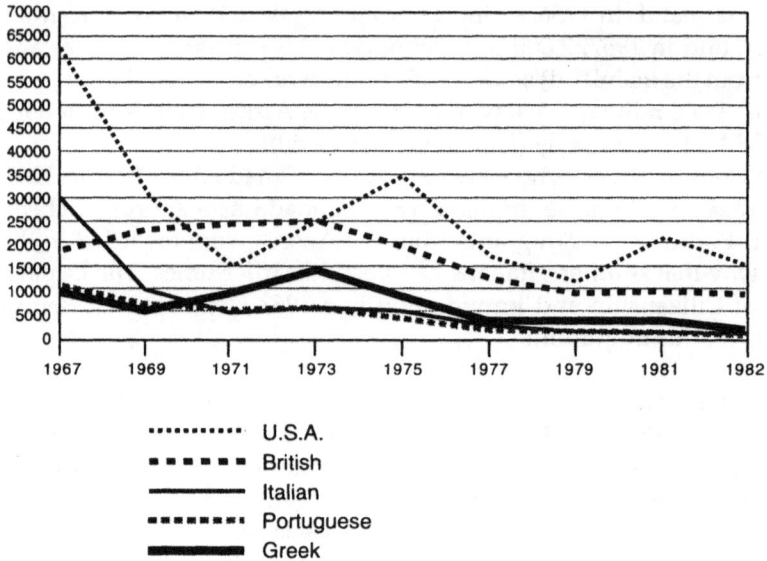

············ U.S.A.
■ ■ ■ ■ ■ ■ British
———————— Italian
■■■■■■■· Portuguese
▬▬▬▬▬▬ Greek

*By country of former residence

Source: Department of Citizenship and Immigration, Department of Manpower
and Immigration, and Employment and Immigration. Immigration Statistics,
1967–82

Figure 2.2. Portuguese Migration to Canada: Comparison to Other Select
Immigrant Groups,* 1967–82

dependent relatives. The latter (called 'nominated relatives') were judged
in part on the same points system as independent applicants.

   Compared to other immigrant groups that have entered Canada, the
Portuguese represent a small, but significant number. In the period that
spans the height of their migration (1967–82), Portuguese were among
the more numerous groups immigrating to Canada, ranking fourth
among all immigrants, and representing over 4 per cent of total migration (Departments of Citizenship and Immigration 1967–82) (see Figure
2.2). After the late 1970s, the numbers of Portuguese entering Toronto
and Canada began to drop sharply (Statistics Canada 1986).

   From 1963 to 1982, 50,960 Portuguese entered Canada as workers
(professional and non-professional), 37 per cent of the total Portuguese
immigration during those two decades (see Tables 2.1, 2.2, and Figure
2.3). The problem with these statistics is that they do not give us a

TABLE 2.1.
The Intended Occupation (Professional/Non-professional) of Portuguese Immigrant*
Workers as a Percentage of Total Portuguese Immigrant Workers in Canada, 1963–82

Professional workers**		Non-professional workers***		Total Portuguese workers	
N	%	N	%	N	%
3,768	7.3	47,192	92	50,960	99.3

*Those whose last country of permanent residence was Portugal.
**Includes male and female managerial, administrative, technical workers, scientists, teachers, health professionals, lawyers, clerical, transportation and communication trade workers, and commercial and financial sales workers.
***Includes service and recreation workers, farmers, loggers, fishers, hunters, trappers, miners, construction trades, manufacturing, and mechanical labourers.
Source: Departments of Citizenship and Immigration, Manpower and Immigration, and Employment and Immigration. Immigration Statistics, 1962–82.

TABLE 2.2.
Total Portuguese Immigrant* Workers and Non-workers as a Percentage of Total
Portuguese Immigration to Canada, 1963–82

Total workers**		Total non-workers***		Total Portuguese immigrants	
N	%	N	%	N	%
50,960	37	86,086	62	137,046	99

*Those whose last country of permanent residence was Portugal.
**Includes both professional and non-professional workers as defined for Table 2.1.
***Wives or spouses (sic), children, and others. This category changed from 'non-workers' to 'not destined for the labour force' in 1980.
Source: Departments of Citizenship and Immigration, Manpower and Immigration, and Employment and Immigration. Immigration Statistics, 1962–82.

gender breakdown (i.e., non-workers are defined in a sexist way as 'wives, spouses, children and others' or as 'not destined for the labour force').

Canadian policies of family reunification in the 1960s brought women and children in large numbers to join their male relatives (see Figure 2.3). The total number of those who entered as non-workers, not destined for the labour force, was 86,086 for the period from 1963–82, 62 per cent of the total Portuguese immigration for that period (see Table 2.2). Most of this category were women and children. In fact, more Portuguese women of working age (20–64 years old) have come to Canada than Portuguese men (see Figure 2.4). Most of these women did

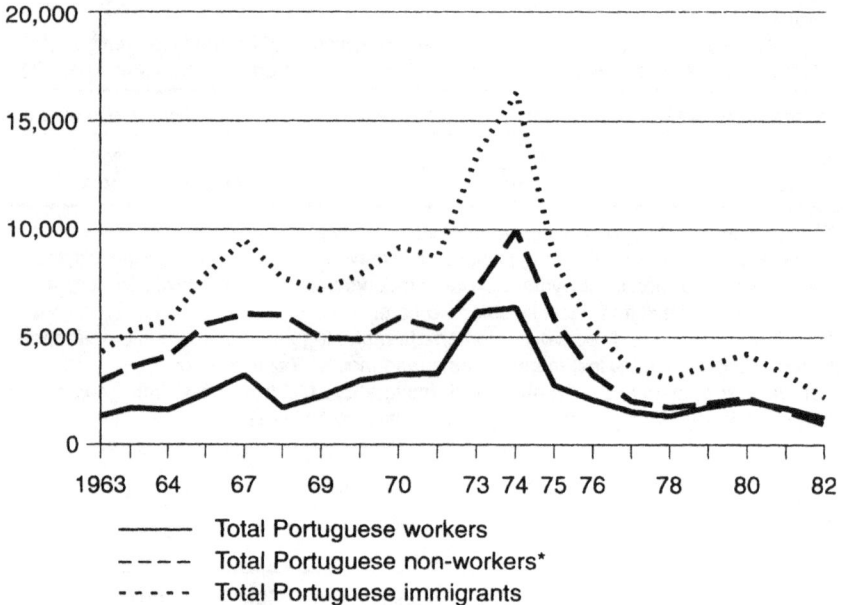

Total Portuguese workers
Total Portuguese non-workers*
Total Portuguese immigrants

Wives or spouses (*sic*), children, and others. This category changed from 'non-workers' to 'not destined for the labour force' in 1980.

Source: Departments of Citizenship and Immigration, Manpower and Immigration, and Employment and Immigration. Immigration Statistics, 1962–82.

Figure 2.3. Portuguese Migration to Canada, 1963–82

not gain entry to Canada as workers, although the majority found paid work after they entered.

The institution of the points system in 1967 favoured male, educated, and professional immigrants. A small number of highly skilled technicians and white-collar Portuguese workers had already begun to migrate to Canada (see Table 2.1). They represented 7.3 per cent of the total Portuguese migration from 1963–82. Anderson and Higgs describe this group as predominantly men who opened up businesses such as travel agencies, or who became real estate agents or driving school instructors in urban centres (1976:44), bringing with them dependent wives or families or sending for them later. These middle-class Portuguese men disassociated themselves both geographically and socially from their working-class compatriots. Many moved to the suburbs directly upon arrival, thus isolating themselves from Portuguese associations and most of the working-class Portuguese people who

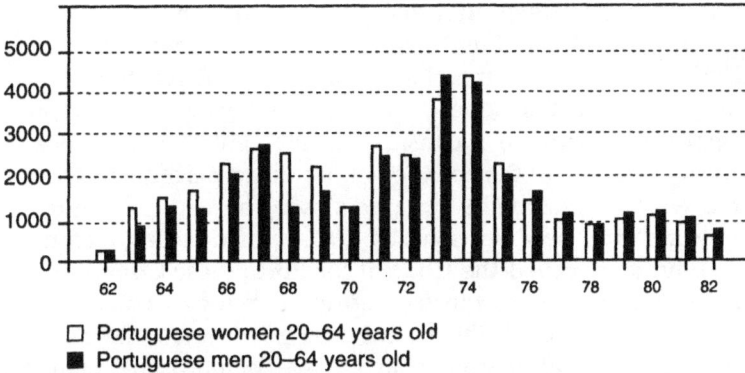

☐ Portuguese women 20–64 years old
■ Portuguese men 20–64 years old

*Country of last permanent residence

Note: Total number of women of working age: 40,150; total number of men of working age: 37,025

Source: Department of Citizenship and Immigration, Department of Manpower and Immigration, and Employment and Immigration. Immigration Statistics, 1962–82

Figure 2.4. Portuguese Immigrant* Women and Men of Working Age Entering Canada, 1962–82

were located in the downtown core (Anderson and Higgs 1976:50). The majority of middle-class and well-educated immigrants were from the Portuguese mainland. Thus, class differences are interwoven with regional differences in this period of migration.[8]

Until November 1973, visitors to Canada were able to apply to become immigrants from within Canada. After that date, immigration regulations stipulated that immigration applications could not be made while resident in Canada. The effects of this change are evident in the sharp drop in numbers of Portuguese immigrants immediately after 1974 (see Figure 2.3). It is significant that Portuguese immigration to Canada was at its height when official multicultural policy was being established in this country (see Figure 2.1), and that Portuguese were among the last group of European immigrants to enter Canada in large numbers.[9]

Before the social democratic revolution of 1974, large numbers of Portuguese left Portugal in clandestine ways and in many cases entered other countries, such as Canada, in the same manner. The revolution in Portugal marked the end of a forty-year dictatorial period, and stiff emigration controls were removed at that time (Rocha-Trindade 1993:266).

The post-revolutionary legislative and policy changes not only opened the doors to emigration, thus legitimating what already existed in practice, but went much farther. New Portuguese citizenship policies opened and extended Portuguese borders. The Portuguese state, in a clearly opportunistic move – considering the central importance of emigrants' remittances to the economy – bestowed permanent and extensive citizenship rights on its emigrants living abroad, including the right to vote in Portuguese elections. By 1981, a Portuguese government advisory committee, called the Council for Portuguese Communities, had been established, with elected representatives in communities abroad (ibid. 267). In 1985, the Portuguese government department responsible for emigration was renamed the Secretariat of State for Portuguese Communities and given a mandate to strengthen bilateral relationships between Portuguese in Portugal and those living abroad (ibid.). The Portuguese government declared Portugal to be a 'global nation' (Feldman-Bianco 1992, 1994), and its emigrants as well as their children were defined as Portuguese. Portuguese emigration policy states:

> To all [citizens] is granted the right of emigrating or leaving the national territory and the right of returning to it. (Article 44 of the Constitution, April 1976, cited in Rocha-Trindade 1993:266) ...

> Portuguese citizens who are or who reside abroad, enjoy the protection of the [Portuguese] State for the exercise of their rights and are liable to the duties which are not incompatible with their absence from the country. (Article 14 of the Constitution, April 1976, ibid.)

This transnational definition of identity reflects the self-interest of Portuguese state economics and politics, and cultural protectionism, as well as a kind of diasporic consciousness on the part of Portugal and the Portuguese (described further in Chapter 6).[10]

Remittances, Return, and Regionalism

One of the most important and well-recognized ways in which immigrants confirm their association with their home country is by sending money to family members or as investments in land, housing, or business ventures. These remittances are greatly encouraged by Portugal, and have been described as 'an important source of foreign exchange, removing a potentially binding foreign exchange constraint ... [that has allowed] ... the purchase of strategic imports during the development process' (Chaney 1986:3). They have been characterized as a 'substitute,' making up for lost income resulting from the lack of development of the Portuguese agricultural sector. Portuguese emigrants, unable to support their households from their agricultural labour, from the mid-1960s to 1970s and onwards, poured out of the rural agricultural regions to the industrialized centres of the world (ibid.), sending money back to Portugal to support those left behind. From 1973 to 1979, emigrant remittances were 8.2 per cent of the gross domestic product, and between 1980 and 1989 this total rose to 10 per cent of GDP (Baganha 1998:201). During the 1980s, remittances were the most important source of foreign currency, approximately US $2 billion per year (Rocha-Trindade 1993:273).

Remitting funds to the homeland is also a gendered phenomenon, demonstrating women's commitment to supporting the basic needs of their families ahead of their personal requirements (Stasiulis and Bakan 1997:131). Stasiulis and Bakan's conclusions (and my own) indicate that immigrant women are staunch in their dedication to remit funds to their families in Portugal. Although my data do not demonstrate definitively that women tend to remit to their mothers rather than to other members of their families (ibid.), it is clear that mothers and wives were more likely than husbands and fathers to nurture family networks, and this commitment usually involved sending money. Some women also owned houses and apartments in Portugal on their own. However, Portuguese state policies demonstrate little understanding of the gendered nature of remittances, at both the giving and receiving ends of the relationship.

It is significant for analyses of Portuguese nationalism that there is a considerable regional differentiation to the remittances received in Portugal. For example, data gathered on regional emigration compared with regional remittances demonstrates that: 1) during the 1970s and 1980s, proportionately more emigrants from the north coast of Portugal (Viana, Braga, and Porto) and centre coast (Aveiro, Coimbra, and Leiria), emigrating to Europe and North and South America, chose to remit monies to their home regions; 2) by the 1980s, Azoreans, migrating mainly to North America, were sending back smaller remittances than emigrants from the north coast, centre coast, or Madeira (Chaney 1986:123,132).

These data correspond to the results of my research on return migration from Toronto to Portugal, which indicated higher return migration rates for Portuguese from the mainland of Portugal than from the Azores.[11] Together, these two sets of data imply, not surprisingly, that those who decide to remain in Canada are more likely to invest their savings in this country than in Portugal. There has been little analysis of the implications of this finding for Canadian immigration policy. Other factors involved in deciding to return to Portugal include the possession of land and other immobile capital in Portugal, the number of family relatives left behind, the availability of other assets (e.g., public services), all of which indicate the social and economic aspects of nationalism and the heterogeneity of the Portuguese immigration to Canada.

Portuguese nationalist 'homeland' policies and practices have gender implications that are demonstrated in the divergent views about returning to Portugal held by men and women in Toronto. The decision to return is based on gendered experiences in the homeland as well as in the country of immigration. Despite the fact that Portuguese women in Toronto are among the groups most likely to be affected by economic restructuring, due to their location in industries most vulnerable to restructuring (Preston and Giles 1997), they are more likely than Portuguese men to want to remain in Canada.[12] In Toronto, non-economic, familial, and personal factors have been the primary reasons for wishing to return, rather than economic or occupational factors. However, as the Canadian economy restructures and that of Portugal improves, Portuguese immigrants and their children have begun to refer to economic factors as also being related to their decision to return. My research in Toronto indicates a variety of views on returning to Portugal from Canada, relating to region of origin, gender, and class. Azorean women are more likely to want to stay in Toronto, and have a pragmatic view of their lives in Portugal:

> In Canada, that's where I suffered. But I never wanted to go back because I know that in Portugal, I would have to work in the fields. And I used to tell my mother [who wanted me to return] 'Please understand: to go back and work on the fields as a labourer, I might as well stay here and make some money. And here I can even send you money! (Januaria, first-generation, cleaner, Azores)

Women from the mainland are more apt to express a desire to return to Portugal, and are more likely to own a house or apartment there (sometimes more than one). Most men from both the Azores and the main-land want to return to Portugal, and some do, even going so far as to leave their wives behind, but then yearn for their care when in Portugal.[13] The husband of one woman made a rather puzzling statement to his wife:

> My husband has a rented apartment in Oporto and he told me, 'You can stay with me, you can cook for me, wash my clothes and I will look after you.' (Laurinda, cleaner, first-generation, mainland)

Portuguese Women and Migration

Portuguese men were more visible than women in early Portuguese migration. However, women have been centrally involved in migration in a variety of ways. Married and unmarried women who remained in Portugal while men emigrated worked harder than ever to care singlehandedly for their children and other dependent relatives, and to maintain family homes, businesses, and farms. Brettell describes the central role of women as agriculturalists in the Minho region of northern mainland Portugal, where a large number of households were headed by women during the nineteenth century and the first half of the twentieth century (1986:137,155). Male emigration has also been linked to the development of women-centred households, in which women's ties were mainly with their matri-kin (Cole 1991:63). It is unlikely that remittances from unskilled male migrant labourers during the early years of the migration adequately made up for the loss of their labour and support to their households in Portugal.

Portuguese immigrant women who came to Canada played a central role in deciding whether and where to migrate. The majority of women interviewed for this book indicated they used their kinship networks in Canada to arrange sponsorship, housing, and jobs for themselves and their husbands. Higgs asserts that Portuguese migration to Canada has been almost entirely a chain migration: applicants without prior contacts constituted less than 5 per cent of new arrivals (1982:6). Combining Higgs's data with my own demonstrates the important influence of women on the Portuguese migration to Canada.[14]

Women also have been major actors in determining 'how' to emigrate, which includes travels through the bureaucratic webs in Portugal: 'They are the ones who walk, hitchhike in from isolated rural

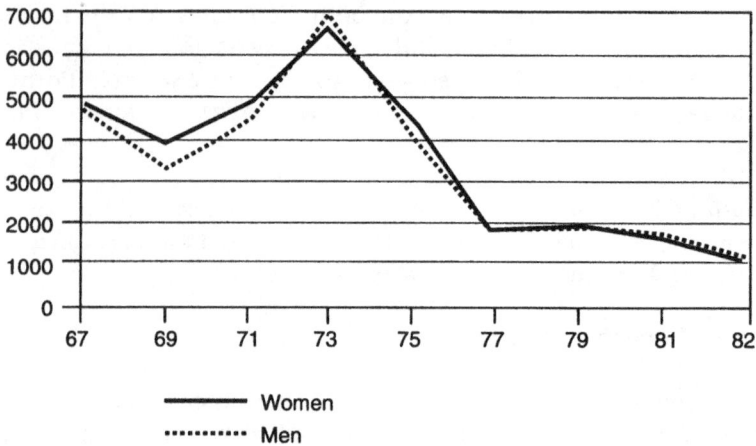

By country of former residence

Source: Department of Citizenship and Immigration, Department of Manpower and Immigration, and Employment and Immigration. Immigration Statistics, 1967–82

Figure 2.5. Portuguese Migration (from Portugal) to Canada by Gender, 1967–82

areas, or take interminable bus trips to spend interminable waits in offices to get papers written, papers signed, certificates prepared and documents stamped' (Smith 1980:82).

The migration of Portuguese women to Canada began in the post-World War II period of the mid-1950s (Anderson and Campbell Davis: 1990). Thus, their settled presence now spans more than forty years and two to three generations. Figure 2.5 indicates that during the fifteen years between 1967–82, Portuguese women came in numbers almost equal to men.

By the early 1960s, there were more Portuguese women of working age arriving in Canada than men. It is significant that, during the two decades from 1962–82, the numbers of Portuguese immigrants of adult working age (20–64 years old) who entered Canada were dominated by women overall and in most years (see Figure 2.4). By combining these quantitative data with my own qualitative data, which indicate that most Portuguese immigrant women began working soon after their arrival, it is clear that the economic contribution of Portuguese immigrant women was crucial to their households and is as important as that of Portuguese men's. Multiple sources of income, from men, women, children, and boarders, are described by Anderson and Higgs as the means by which Portuguese households in Canada retained family homes and survived through difficult economic times (1976:45). Portuguese immigrant women traditionally are described as hard-working women who often look for wage work in the days immediately following their arrival in Canada. Women and children picked worms to sell for fishing bait, and women often worked two or more jobs in the cleaning industry and in factories to support the household, in many cases sacrificing their limited opportunities to learn English or upgrade their skills.[15]

Although the poorer treatment that women received in Canada as sponsored immigrants, and the gender relations of the Portuguese family led Portuguese immigrant women, and some of their daughters, to work in low-paying, unskilled jobs in cleaning and factory work, they often struggled against their working conditions through membership in labour unions and labour activism (Neal and Neale 1987; Neal 1994). Marques and Medeiros (1980) describe the important role that Portuguese women workers played in the 1970s in the cleaning industry and in a factory struggle to ameliorate working conditions (see Chapter 4).

The daughters of these first-generation women are located in a broader spectrum of wage work than their mothers. Their fluency in English, and their high school, college, or university education have enabled many to move into white collar jobs, or in their mother's words, 'clean jobs.' Many of these women want to be recognized as different from their mothers, whom they regard as having been stereotyped as 'passive and lacking in skills and creativity' (Borreicho and Ferreira 1992:G7). They argue that Portuguese women are now establishing themselves 'in all the major fields and professions,' while 'also playing a major role in maintaining family unity and fostering a supportive environment' (ibid.). The experiences that they and their families have lived through are a result of an intense relocation and realignment of resources in both Portugal and Canada. During this time, national and international restructuring has shaped and reshaped the Canadian immigration landscape. In the next chapter, I pursue this exploration through the stories of four Portuguese women from several households in Toronto.

Chapter Three

Culture, Politics, and Resistance in the Household[1]

This chapter explores the experience of Portuguese women and men in households that are undergoing transformation, responding to internal life cycles, as well as to the external demands of the Canadian and international economy, politics, and culture. The experiences of first- and second-generation Portuguese women and men – the first generation coming from villages, towns, and cities in Portugal and recreating households in Toronto, and the second generation, loosening the household bonds so carefully tended by their parents and remaking other 'homes' – are the fabric of this exploration.

Through the stories of four women, I critique homogeneous notions of Portuguese households or homes and the experiences of the men, women, and children who inhabit them. I examine the differences and commonalities between and within Portuguese households and across generations. Some excellent migration literature describes the difficulties experienced by second-generation women living with a foot in two cultures.[2] Naturalized and confining images of what it is to be a Portuguese immigrant woman continue to create serious tensions for first-generation women. These women, more than the second-generation, engage in the difficult task of both remembering their cultural history and re-membering or remaking the Portuguese household in Toronto in light of this history.

Households exist for the survival of their members, across time and, in the case of immigrants and migrants, across countries and continents. Households are economic enterprises unto themselves, but are linked to other households, and always shaped by the larger economy and culture in which they are embedded. Their linkages to other households may be economic, but are also affective, involving community and family associations. The Portuguese household networks described by Grace Anderson (1974) depict the ways in which relationships across continents have evolved into migrations of entire families and sometimes whole villages of men, women, and children. These networks have been used to ensure that household members find jobs and housing, as well as access to information essential to orienting them to their new neighbourhood and community. International linkages to Portugal remain a permanent and integral part of the household for Portuguese first-generation immigrants. An orientation to return to Portugal, whether in fact they ever do, is often inherent in the way members of first-generation households define themselves.

The ideology of the *casa* (household), and of returning to the *casa* in Portugal, is described by de Pina-Cabral (1986) as central to the ideology of Portuguese migration. Most immigrant households retain their ties to the home country, leaving their community and business affairs to relatives to ensure they remain in good standing when they return (de Pina-Cabral 1986:80). De Pina-Cabral writes that when Portuguese migrants, like Portuguese in their home country, refer to *minha casa* (my household), they have 'both the people and the land in mind' (1984:78). This household is the unit of commensality, residence, and management of production for the peasants from northern Portugal that he describes.

Household Gender Relations

The economics of the household are interwoven with ideologies of family that culturally define appropriate roles for men, women, and children. Here again, generational differences, as well as gendered and other differences, are shaped by the disparate experiences of the two generations of Portuguese in Toronto. Family ideologies include concepts such as appropriate gender identity of the economic provider(s), appropriate behaviour and personality for males and females and, by extension, appropriate domestic gender roles and tolerated levels of parental authority. The considerable variation across generations of Portuguese in Toronto in definitions of family and in family ideologies is related at least in part to the varying impact of the hegemonic culture on different generations of immigrants.

Portuguese first-generation women in Toronto are located in households that have been reconstructed and defined for the most part by the Canadian immigration policy of family reunification. Thus, immigration status for young and elderly dependants in a family has been based on historically evolving criteria including age, biological relationship, and disability. Portuguese women, like women from other ethnic groups, have entered Canada principally as dependants of men and were defined officially as not being destined for the labour force. While this means that Portuguese women have been allowed to enter Canada as permanent settlers, it has also led to their differential treatment in Canadian settlement policies and by employers, which has contributed to an underclass of immigrant workers in Canada. Second-generation women are expected by their parents to remain in the parental household until they marry, and many find this degree of parental control extremely difficult. But for some, this difficulty is outweighed by financial considerations: the attractive possibility of being able to save sufficient funds to invest in a house of one's own upon marriage. Depending upon the household's economic circumstances, working children may not be expected to contribute proportionately to the household economy, but to save for their future. Keeping their children under their roof enables parents to exert a certain degree of control over them, but it also provides the children with a kind of dowry that working-class parents are often unable to provide. Needless to say, the only acceptable route out of these households is via heterosexual marriage.

Second-generation households are a terrain of resistance for women against the traditional gender relations promoted in the homes of first-generation parents. Second-generation women all speak of the different treatment accorded them compared to their brothers:

> I find that Portuguese families feel that men are not the same as women. They kind of think of it, 'Well, he's a male and there's no problem.' But a female, it does cause more of a problem – more of a disrespect. And they're afraid of what other people might think. (Emilia, second-generation, office manager, Azores)

One woman referred to the 'traditional Portuguese son act' in describing the position of honour accorded her brothers in the family:

> There is nothing worse than to have a single mother with five daughters and two sons. The eldest of which is a boy, her pride and joy. This is the man who is going to get his coffee brought to him, that is going to be catered to and still is, in many ways. The youngest [son] is the baby. He's the one that she's forever taking care of. Whenever things were doled out,

those two would get preference. The women were always fighting for what we could get. (Rosa, second-generation, community worker, Azores)

These women express feelings of being controlled and of being held in positions of low esteem. This perception is related directly to the threat they represent to the family's reputation, as carriers of family virtue. In the majority of cases, they describe their fathers as being most concerned with their daughters' sexual and social freedom, although their mothers play an important enforcement role. The greatest fear is that a daughter might become pregnant before marriage, although for many, this may be condoned, so long as the marriage occurs immediately and takes place in the church. What may be seen as worse, as one second-generation informant noted, is not marrying in the church, or waiting too long after marriage to have a child.

The resistance of second-generation women to unequal gender relations in the household varies. There are households in which men are expected to do half the housework. However, most second-generation women speak about men as helpers in the household, while women are helpers in tasks outside the house, such as washing the car and gardening. Second-generation women who work at wage jobs may offload their domestic labour onto their mothers' shoulders. Although these women are often critical of their mothers' double burden, they also regard this work as something first-generation women are used to doing:

She doesn't really have much time for herself [and] always wants to keep on the go. She babysits her grandchildren, including my son. She takes care of my grandmother who is ninety-four. She makes sure that supper's made when my dad comes home, the ironing is done, the house is clean. She also does all the banking. So I find that she has a lot more chores than I do during the day because my main role is coming to work. I do my job but I don't find that I'm under as much pressure as mom is per se. (Lucinda, second-generation, office supervisor, Azores)

Notions of household and family require definition across generations as well as within generations of Portuguese in Toronto. Gender, class, region of origin, and other differences play a significant part in this definition. Empirical case studies of three households provide a deeper understanding of household survival strategies and decision-making among the Portuguese in Toronto.

Three Portuguese Households in Toronto

The following case studies were not chosen for their representativeness. They demonstrate the complexity and variability among households of Portuguese in Toronto, but also include some underlying elements that are common across Portuguese households.

The first case describes the established household of Januaria, a first-generation woman, and the second, the household of Helena, a second-generation woman. The third case combines the stories of a first-generation mother, Suzana, and her second-generation daughter, Felicidade. Table 3.1 compares the social characteristics and immigration history of each woman, and Table 3.2 illustrates a life history of each woman, in which comparisons can be made by year and age.

Januaria's Household
Januaria, 39 years old
Julio, husband, 49 years old
Mary, daughter, 18 years old
Anna, daughter, 16 years old
Anthony, son, 13 years old
Christina, daughter, 9 years old

Januaria, born on the Azorean island of São Miguel, arrived with her mother in Toronto in the winter of 1969 (see Table 3.1) when she was seventeen years old. Their trip was to have been a temporary visit to see her brother and a sister and to find short-term jobs. Having incurred debts from paying for dowries for two other daughters in Portugal, Januaria's mother was combining a family visit with a stint at what, by Portuguese standards of the time, was considered a well-paid job in a Toronto factory.

A year and a half later, with her debts paid off, Januaria's mother was ready to return to Portugal. She left for São Miguel, dismayed that Januaria, her youngest child, would not return with her. The income from a job in a plant nursery and the freedom she experienced living in Toronto persuaded Januaria to stay, but not without regrets. As time progressed, she settled permanently in Toronto, but felt ambivalent about the family life she had left in Portugal. Her relationships with her siblings in Canada became conflictual, distanced, and aloof:

I really missed my life as a single woman in Portugal. In Portugal I never

TABLE 3.1
Case Studies: Social Characteristics and Immigration Histories of Four Women

Name	Gener-ation	Place of Birth	Age at Time of Interview	Year of Immigra-tion to Canada	Marital Status	Children	Education	English Fluency	Employment at Time of Interview	Household Income
Januaria	First	Azores	39	1969	Married	3 daughters, 1 son	2 years	Working knowledge	Unemployed (had been a cleaner)	Unknown
Helena	Second	Azores	36	1967	Common-law	1 daughter	College graduate	Fluent	Community worker	$25,000
Suzana	First	Rural northern Portugal	55	1969	Married	1 daughter, 1 son	4 years + Beautician course	Fluent	Beautician	$12,000
Felicidade	Second	Lisbon	27	1969	Engaged	None	College graduate	Fluent	Secretary	$25,000

went lacking for anything, even though my mother had eight children. We never went hungry. We never had any great unhappiness. We never fought. We got along well and we lived very well.

The period after her mother left Canada was stressful for Januaria, who moved between her sister's home and that of the sister of her new fiancé. Living with her fiancé was out of the question morally and they could not afford two apartments. Finally, Januaria's mother became exasperated with her children's quarrels, and, insisting that her daughter should not be living with 'strangers' (her fiancé's family), she flew back to Toronto to share an apartment with Januaria until she married.

Strained as these relationships may have become at times, the support of her relatives was invaluable to Januaria in settling in Toronto. She participated in different types of households, first as a single woman, then married, then with children. She and her husband bought their own home in 1986 (see Table 3.2). Ties with her mother in Portugal were particularly important to Januaria's settlement in Toronto. Her mother worked hard at her familial relations, moving back and forth between Portugal and Canada to ensure that her engaged daughter remained a respectable Portuguese woman in Toronto.

Over the course of twenty years, Januaria gave birth to four children and moved in and out of the workforce as a horticultural factory worker and cleaner. Her engagement in wage work caused arguments with Julio, who maintained from the time their first daughter was born that, 'It's up to the mother to look after her children. Not somebody else.' Despite these protests, on several occasions when Julio was laid off from his work, Januaria's salary was the sole household income.

There are contradictions between Januaria's paid work and her home life. She is firm that both her own and her daughters' primary attachment should be to the home: 'Women were meant to stay home and men were made to be out.' However, this does not include wage work. Januaria points out that 'women who stay home are criticized.' But criticism or not, the last thing that Januaria wished to give up was a paid job. She wanted to 'bring home a pay-cheque, and get a bit of distraction and entertainment ... to work, to laugh, to talk.' But she also contends that, 'A woman should be what her husband tells her to be.' Yet, when describing how her husband resented her working outside the house, her response was that, 'I had to work anyway.'

Over the course of her marriage to Julio, he had various jobs in the construction industry that resulted in serious injuries to his neck, hands, and other parts of his body, requiring stitches, surgery, and lengthy recuperation periods. Januaria cared for him when he was released from the hospital, while tending to the children and going to work, a common experience for many Portuguese first-generation women whose spouses work in construction and manual labour. Their domestic arrangements are often strained by workplace accidents:

> We've had a life with its bitter moments. I had to go to the hospital, I still had to cook for the kids. I used to ride home at nine, go to bed without eating. And then he came home and had to be in bed for awhile. He couldn't move, but I could only spend two days with him and then I had to go back to the factory.

Of the four children, three girls and a boy, the two older girls dropped out of high school before finishing. The two youngest children were still in elementary school at the time of the interview. The story of Mary, the eldest, is revealing of the difficulties that Portuguese families confront in Canada. At fourteen, Mary complained to her parents that she was being sexually harassed by a male teacher, but Julio, perhaps not wanting to believe that his daughter's honour was in jeopardy, ignored both her and her mother's pleas:

> My husband is the kind of man if you tell him, 'Well that teacher doesn't like Mary,' he'll say, 'That's because she's up to no good.' And she cried so much. She used to say, 'I'm not misbehaving in school, Daddy. That teacher puts his arms on my shoulders and I don't like that. And I can't stand him.'

Mary began to object to the teacher's advances and was transferred to a school that she considered to be an institution for 'low achievement kids.' She felt out of place and lost interest in her classes. At fifteen, she skipped school for six months, meeting friends in a donut shop before her parents were made aware of her absence by the school. Her father expressed the most anger and humiliation. He was particularly upset that she might have been 'wandering around the city.' He marched her back to the donut shop to 'prove' to him that this was not the case. He said, 'I won't kill her, but I've got to teach her a lesson. She's not a baby anymore.' But when they reached the donut shop, he said, 'I'm not going in because I'm ashamed. If that couple [the owners] knows that you've been here from morning until night, what will they think of me?'

The next day, Januaria and Mary had a meeting at the school. The experience of Januaria, a woman with little English and two years of schooling, negotiating her daughter's future with what she described as a daunting roomful of 'higher authorities,' speaks volumes about the struggles of immigrants to access education for themselves and their children. Mary left school that day and started cleaning in a department store. When that job ended a few months later, a former teacher convinced her to go back to the school and enter the hairdressing course. Her younger sister, Anna, following a path similar to Mary's, was absent from school for two months before her parents found out. She told her parents that she didn't like school, and at sixteen she left to work as a cashier. Since leaving, Anna has reconsidered her limited options and is now trying to finish high school by correspondence while she works.

Although the daughters in the family are still living at home and contributing to household expenses on an ad hoc basis, their unpaid labour is central to the household. Although Januaria contends that, 'Everybody works the same here at home,' Julio and their son are outside this circle. Januaria and her daughters disagree about their brother's lack of involvement in domestic chores:

> My daughters tell their brother, 'Make your bed.' And I tell them, 'No, in Portugal my brothers didn't do any housework.' And they say, 'Well, in Canada men have to learn how to do these things.' I say, 'No, they'll learn by themselves.'

Januaria is constantly negotiating with her husband concerning both her role and her children's. She says the children are 'very afraid' of their father, and spend more time talking with her, telling her their problems and plans. Despite the hardships Januaria has experienced over the years in Toronto, like many immigrants, she views her migration as a successful economic decision.

Helena's Household
Helena, 36 years old
Ilda, daughter, 5 years old
Michael, common-law husband

Helena, a second-generation Portuguese woman, spent eleven years on the island of São Miguel before coming to Toronto (see Table 3.2).

She describes these years as central to her sense of being Portuguese in Canada:

I wouldn't be the kind of person I am today if I hadn't had the experience of having been Portuguese in the village where I was brought up.

She describes being raised in a predominatly female community in Portugal, living among her mother, aunts, grandmother, and other women of the village, many of whom had husbands who had migrated elsewhere for work. Helena's father had come to Canada on a Canadian government contract to build railroads in the 1950s, and she saw little of him until the family rejoined him in Toronto in 1967 (see Table 3.1). The migration of Helena's family to Toronto was initiated mainly to prevent her two brothers from being drafted into the Portuguese army to fight in the African colonial wars.[3]

The schoolroom predominated among Helena's first experiences in Toronto. Attending a downtown Toronto Catholic school, in the mid-1960s, Helena remembers that 90 per cent of the students were Portuguese, and that many of them, like herself, were unable to speak English. Because of her lack of English, she was demoted to a grade four class:

The only thing I understood was math. But my impression at that point was that I had been put in a class of retarded kids, because the grade 4 in Portugal, the math, was much more advanced than math in grade 4 here. So I'd come home and cry that I was in a retarded class. That was my first year in school. That was the strongest impression. I felt stupid.

In contrast to the 'library on wheels' that visited her village once a week in Portugal, Helena describes being 'totally impressed' by the school library in Toronto, which became a magnet for her as soon as she learned to read English. She read 'like a maniac' in her grade school and continued to devour literature into her high school years, to the worry of her barely literate parents:

I'd stay up until two or three in the morning, reading. My mother would get very worried that I was losing my eyesight, and that I shouldn't read so much, that I'd have a mental breakdown. And she'd come into my room and turn off the light. So I'd do it undercover, under the blankets, so she couldn't detect the light under the door.

It wasn't until she was in her last year of high school that Helena realized she would have no hope of entering university to pursue her interest in literature unless she repeated grades 12 and 13. Helena had been streamed, like so many of her Portuguese friends, into a commercial school. She was discouraged from entering the business administration/secretarial program at a polytechnical institute by her school principal, who told her that in spite of her 'A' average, her English would not be acceptable. Helena persevered, was accepted at the polytechnic, and completed four years of post-secondary education there. She then decided she did not want to be a secretary and soon after, left Canada to travel in Latin America for a year and a half.

When she returned, Helena decided to move from her parents' home to an apartment of her own. She describes how doing this was far worse for her mother than the fact that she had spent more than a year travelling, because at least then, 'you aren't in the country.' The day she moved from her parents' home

> was like a burial. The neighbours, who were also from our village, came to our house and wailed as if a person had died. The women tried to stop me physically from going out. It was horrible! And my mother had an attack, she passed out. She had diabetes and they were trying to guilt me into believing that I had killed my mother. I was twenty-four. My mother died of a heart attack a year and a half later and as much as you know it isn't true, there is always a bit of doubt left within you. So there was always guilt involved.

Speaking Portuguese, English, and Spanish fluently, and feeling a strong commitment to the immigrant community, particularly her own, Helena found a job as a community worker. This was by no means her first job; she had worked since she was fourteen years old as a cleaner and a factory worker (see Table 3.2).

Marriage had never been a goal for Helena, and she attributes this to her experience in Portugal, living in a household and a community dominated by women. She perceived a great contrast between her life in Portugal and her parents' household in Toronto. In Portugal:

> work was shared among women. Now looking on it, I think my mother had a lot more control over her own life without my father around, than after we came here and started living with him. And we never felt alone – other women either single or whose husbands were away and had no

TABLE 3.2
Case Studies: Life Histories of Four Women

Year	Januaria	Helena	Suzana	Felicidade
1952	Born (Azores)			
1953	1		Enters convent	
1954	2	Father emigrates to Canada	17	
1955	3	Born (Azores)	18	
1956	4	Lives with grandmother and aunt	19	
1957	Begins working on father's land	2	Leaves convent to work in factory in Lisbon and attend night school 20	
1958	6	3	Promotion to work in factory cafeteria and shipping/receiving	
1959	7	4	22	
1960	School	5	Marries	
1961	School	6	Finishes beautician course	
1962	Works on family farm	7	25	
1963	11	School; begins to live with mother	Son is born	
1964	12	School	Daughter is born	Born in Lisbon
1965	13	School	Self-employed as chiropodist and seamstress	1
1966	14	School	29	2
1967	15	12 Migrates to Toronto with mother, rejoins father; school	30	3

TABLE 3.2 *(Continued)*
Case Studies: Life Histories of Four Women

Year	Januaria	Helena	Suzana	Felicidade
1968	'Fiancé' in Portugal mother doesn't like	School	31	4
1969	Migrates to Toronto with mother; job in plant nursery	School; joins church youth group; part-time cleaner	Migrates to Toronto with husband and 2 children; job with beautician company; begins volunteer activities in Portuguese community	Migrates with parents and brother to Toronto
1970	Factory job	Streamed to commercial school	33	Starts school in Toronto
1971	Mother returns from Portugal to live with her until she marries	School	34	7
1972	20	School, part-time factory work	Buys house in Toronto; becomes self-employed as beautician.	Fails grade due to language problems
1973	First daughter born; stops working	18/Polytechnical – secretarial course	36	9
1974	Office cleaning job	19	37	10
1975	Second daughter born	20	38	11
1976	Furniture factory job	Secretarial job; leaves to travel	39	12
1977	Son born; long illness; stops working	22	40	13
1978	26	23	41	14

TABLE 3.2 (Continued)
Case Studies: Life Histories of Four Women

Year	Januaria	Helena	Suzana	Felicidade
1979	Returns to furniture factory job	Returns from travels; moves from 'home'; 'leaves' Portuguese community	Cleaning supervisor and self-employd as beautician	15
1980	28	Hospital cleaning job	43	Runs away from home; stays in Children's Aid group home; leaves Catholic girls' school for co-ed public school
1981	Third daughter born	Community worker job	44	Moves back home
1982	Furniture factory job; mother dies in Portugal	Mother dies in Toronto	45	Runs away from home a second time; shares apartment with friend; job selling shoes
1983	31	28	46	Moves back home; finishes high school
1984	32	29	47	Manages an apartment building
1985	33	Common-law relationship	48	Enters college; completes computer course
1986	Buys house	Daughter is born; leaves common-law partner	49	22
1987	Clothing factory job	32	50	Store equipment salesperson
1988	36	33	51	23

TABLE 3.2 (Concluded)
Case Studies: Life Histories of Four Women

Year	Januaria	Helena	Suzana	Felicidade
1989	37	New common-law relationship	52	Secretary
1990	Cleaning job	35	53	25
1991	Unemployed	36	Buys two apartments in Portugal that she is renovating and furnishing	26
1992	40	37	55	Engaged to marry

children, would come over and sleep in our house. So I basically was brought up with a lot of women all around me.

Toronto brought a very different experience that Helena describes as living 'in a household of men':

It became a completely different milieu, where we women served the men, including my brothers. And that was the best feminist learning that you could undergo. I'd say, 'Why do I have to clean up if you are the ones that messed it up?' And my mother would say, 'No, you have to clean it because you're the woman.' That's the point where I decided that I'd never get married.

So when, in her early thirties, Helena found herself pregnant and in a relationship she wanted to leave, she decided to go through with the pregnancy and raise the child as a single parent.

Helena says that, although she has retreated from her former association with the Portuguese community, she has not lacked support:

I have friends whom I have known for years and years and they are like my family. And that's been very important to me. The people who are my family are not even from the [Portuguese] community. They give me concrete help. Sometimes I'm short of money. And they've been there for me.

Helena claims that the relationship that she now has with Michael, her common-law husband, is built on as much equality as possible, in and outside the household:

Any man who comes into my life now, I'm not going to make space for him. He has to make his own space – because if he's going to live there, he's got the same responsibility as me. The great difference in this relationship is that my priority is my daughter and right after that is work. My relationship [with Michael] and my friendships are all on the same level.

Although only three years apart in age, Januaria and Helena seem to be light years apart in their values and attitudes towards gender relations and issues of sexuality in the household. Helena, arriving in Toronto at approximately the same time period, but at a younger age (see Table 3.2), struggled through the education system, never quite achieving the schooling for which she fought, but was still successful in attaining a satisfying, if not highly remunerative, profession. Likewise, Januaria has struggled with the education system, but not on her own behalf. She barely managed to achieve two years of education before leaving Portugal to work in Canada. Her involvement with the Canadian school system has been for the sake of her children, but her efforts so far have not yielded the results she had hoped for her two elder daughters. Like Helena, Januaria has 'always worked,' determined to provide for her household. Both have been employed in factories and as cleaners, traditional jobs for Portuguese women. However, Helena has been able to move beyond these types of work to a 'clean job,' in the words of some first-generation women (Giles 1993).

The type of household in which each woman is located is what most differentiates them. Helena, shunning the traditional Portuguese household and a married relationship, casts back to her early years in Portugal 'in a household run by women' as the formative time of her life. And it is those memories, not necessarily or solely, the 'modernizing' experience of living in Canada, that have moved her beyond the traditional household and family ideologies that she encounters in Toronto, to choose instead a coterie of loyal friends and a common-law partner as her family. Januaria likewise reaches beyond her extended family for support and friendship, and struggles with definitions that her husband and others seek to impose on her, that would exclude her from defining herself as a wage working woman, who has a legitimate place outside the household. However, she also helps the patriarchally defined household survive. Confined by her language abilities, and lack of education and community associations, all of which are intertwined and interdependent, Januaria in many respects leads a more contradictory life than Helena. Helena's freedom to choose the communities with which she associates is related to her education and fluency in English. These advantages have provided her with alternatives which are unavailable to Januaria.

The Household of Suzana and Her Daughter, Felicidade
Suzana, age 55
Carlos, husband, age 55
Martin, son, divorced with son, age 29
Felicidade, daughter, age 27
David, fiancé of Felicidade, age 27

There are both differences and common ground in the way Suzana and her daughter, Felicidade, tell their household history. I begin with Suzana, who initially described her life in the northern region of Portugal as 'very easy and simple as most Portuguese women.' As her story progressed, she began to reveal the more difficult side of her youth and that of other women in Portugal:

> In the mainland the woman is the man's slave. Women work the fields side by side with men, plus she does everything in the house or she could go in the workshop just like I did with my father, and I had to go to the fields, and I had to do housework because my mother was very sick and I was the only daughter.

She attended school for four years, the minimum required in the early 1950s in Portugal. When she was sixteen years old, she left home to enter a convent in Lisbon (see Table 3.2). After four years, she decided that she didn't want to enter the religious life, and left the convent to work in a factory in Lisbon. While working in the factory, she studied for several years at night school to be a beautician. During this time, she met her husband Carlos and gave birth to her two children.

In 1969, the year Suzana and Carlos immigrated to Canada, they both had good jobs in Lisbon. Carlos was employed in a large factory that provided benefits and services to its employees, such as the workplace day care that their children attended every day, and Suzana was building up her clientele in her own business as a beautician. Seeking economic betterment in Canada was not uppermost in their minds:

> When I immigrated it wasn't because of the money, although I had no money there, neither house nor car. It was like everybody else, I spent what I earned – nobody talked about saving. When I decided to come here it was precisely because of the war in Angola, and all the soldiers were being sent to Angola, and none of them would return – all of those that I knew – and I had a son. So I decided that we would get out while he was a child. So my husband had a sister here and asked them to sponsor us.

Suzana and Carlos were met at the Toronto airport and then housed in turn by relatives on both sides in rural areas outside of Toronto. From that point, the sequence of events is characteristic of the ingenuity and resourcefulness of many Portuguese women who come to Canada. The first Monday after she arrived, Suzana arranged a ride with an Azorean grocer who went to Toronto to pick up his supplies once a week. She called an old friend who told her about an apartment that was available next door to her. Finding her way to an employment centre, Suzana found a job within the week as a beautician, and Carlos began to work in construction.

A few years later, through a friend, Suzana found a better job for Carlos in an automobile assembly factory, where he has worked steadily, except for intermittent layoffs. Disliking the cut-throat business of competing for clients and vying for bonuses, Suzana left the beauty company and since then has been mainly self-employed. At times, she has taken on extra jobs, particularly when Carlos is laid off. For two years she worked as a cleaning supervisor in a large factory.

Suzana and Carlos bought a house after three years and paid off the mortgage within ten years. More recently they bought two apartments in Portugal, while downsizing and remortgaging their property in Toronto. With children and grandchildren in Toronto, Suzana envisages that she and her husband will move back and forth between Portugal and Toronto when they retire. But it is her husband who is most eager to return permanently:

He wants to go there because he grew up in the countryside, the rural area, and he loves it. He has a few friends there, not many anymore, but he has his father and he wants to help his father out. If he goes, of course, where my husband goes I go too, but I already have a grandchild here.

Over the years, in addition to her paid work, Suzana has acted as a counsellor in family planning for married couples, as an advocate for elders, and a support for destitute families in various Catholic parishes. Once, when her husband was laid off and on unemployment insurance, she says:

That wasn't enough because our life was organized around his pay cheque. So at that point I had to take on three jobs: I was already self-employed, plus housework; I was working three days with the elder's group that I founded [where] I worked four hours a day, from 10 to 2 p.m. Then I came home for my appointments [as a beautician], and then at 5 p.m. I'd go and work as a cleaning supervisor until past 11 p.m. at night.

Her volunteer work is of central importance:

It's always the case that I will cancel my appointments to do my charitable work and not the other way around because I figure that the other person's hardship is worse than mine.

Carlos supports her activities, and has accompanied her from time to time on an emergency call to help a family. He doesn't complain (at least openly) about her absence from home. And yet Suzana has very traditional values concerning the role of a woman in the household and this is reflected in her marital counselling:

> The woman should dress herself up and look nice for when her husband comes home, to set a beautiful table, to have everything ready for when he comes, so he notices there's more love. A husband who wants to have his wife at night should start preparing her from the morning. A kiss, a bouquet of flowers, notice that there's something different about her when she goes to the hairdresser and vice versa, when the man puts on a nice shirt. To keep a beautiful clean house tidy, that helps a lot.

For Suzana, a satisfying sexual relationship is linked to a gendered division of labour in the home. Indeed, Suzana describes women as destined to do 'everything at home,' because they are 'born with that [domestic] skill.' This is one of the areas in which Suzana and her daughter, Felicidade, disagree. This disagreement is typical of the two generations of Portuguese women:

> Myself and her father too, used to say: 'Do this, it's not men's work,' and I told my daughter, 'You have to do it because you're a woman and he's a man.'

Suzana extends this critique of her daughter, making an association between Felicidade's views on gender equality and sexual relations:

> She's very *machista*, she believes in equality in every way. For example, if a man has the right to have a woman outside, the woman has the same right and I totally and strongly disagree with this, because the man cannot get pregnant.

These and other differences over the years have led to periods of estrangement between Suzana and her daughter, particularly when Felicidade was a teenager. Suzana questions whether her relationship with Felicidade might have been different:

> My mother was very sick too and there was never a relationship like nowadays. I think that marked me a lot. I always try to talk to my daughter at the appropriate times, but if I had to live it again, I would do it

differently. After I reared my children, I read books about kids' education and how to understand child psychology and I learned a great deal after I had already gone through that phase.

Suzana and Carlos's son, Martin, experienced a different home life than his sister. Unlike Felicidade, he was never compelled to do domestic work, and he had far more social freedom. Nor was he encouraged to work outside of the household. Suzana, who studied hard to upgrade her qualifications while an adult in Portugal, had high hopes for her children's education. She says that, against her will, her children started working, and never achieved the education that she had wished for them. Despite tests that identified him as highly intelligent, Martin never went beyond grade nine, and his educational and work history is characterized by recurrent attempts to return to school and to employment:

> Then he wanted to go to school to learn soldering, but he needed grade twelve or grade thirteen; he, who never went beyond grade nine, passed [graduated from high school] with 83 per cent, so he was admitted to trade school. He spent a certain time in that course and then he dropped out too. I was very upset again. Then later on, he passed a test and attended the course of welder/fitter; he passed all the exams and his lowest mark was 95 per cent. He started working and he was so good, bosses were always after him, but he would lose jobs because he would goof off.

Martin's marriage ended in divorce, and his child now lives with his former wife. He was unemployed at the time of the interview.

Felicidade brings a different perspective to the migration of her family to Toronto. She remembers little of Portugal, having arrived in Canada the day before her sixth birthday. Her first years in school in Toronto were difficult as she struggled to master English, never quite catching up to the other students, until she was held back a year in grade three. She was an average student until her early teens, when she began to skip classes. Her parents became increasingly frustrated and angry with her rebelliousness, and tried to frighten her into conforming with their wishes by physically abusing her. By the time she was sixteen, Felicidade was fed up with the discipline and abuse of her home life. A school counsellor, noticing bruises on her legs, offered her the option of living in a group home under the care of Children's Aid.

In a bold move, Felicidade left her home as well as the girls' school, to live in a Children's Aid hostel and enter a co-educational public technical school. Within a year she moved back home again:

It was my dad who was the one that went out looking for me [and convinced me to come home]. So my mother was more the disciplinarian. If there's anybody my friends were scared of it was their fathers. With us it was our mother. She was the strong one.

Felicidade now describes the physical discipline that her parents meted out to their children not as abuse, but as being 'out of love,' a form of punishment she approves of:

You got slapped quite fast and easy but that's the way they were brought up too. It was rare there were bruises left ... their parents did it. I still believe in physical discipline. I won't use any objects ... but a slap on the hand ... a smack on the bum.

Felicidade left her school, ostensibly because she 'got stuck in a class of all girls,' and found a job selling shoes. A year later she ran away from home a second time, and moved into an apartment with a friend. She later reconciled with her parents and moved back home. In another attempt, Felicidade finished high school and entered George Brown College, where she took a computer electronics course. She also worked as an apartment manager and as a store equipment salesperson. Despite setbacks, she has been resourceful in finding employment and continuing her education. Her secretarial work for a large computer company has inspired her to return to school to study accounting.

In our study, we found that the women were employed more consistently than the men they lived with, although usually in a series of jobs over time, as demonstrated both in this household and Januaria's. The women often provide essential ongoing support for the household. As well, women often find jobs for men through their networks, as Suzana did for her household and Felicidade for her fiancé.

Felicidade's network extends to her cousins, with whom she is 'really close,' and to the Portuguese friends that she made through a youth group at the Catholic Church her family attended. But she differentiates between 'the Portuguese community' and her 'Canadianized' Portuguese friends:

This group – they're Portuguese – and they became my really, true friends. We always contact each other and get together still, but my friends are 'Canadianized.' I don't hang around the Portuguese community.

Felicidade is surprised that her parents are not as close to their brothers and sisters as she is to her cousins, having assumed that 'coming to Canada would have brought them closer.'

Now twenty-seven, Felicidade will soon leave home to marry her fiancé, David. Marriage to this non-Portuguese man is viewed by her mother with some indifference. In Suzana's words: *Não fede, nem cheira* (He doesn't stink, but neither does he smell). However, Felicidade says she sought out a non-Portuguese partner to minimize the possibility of violence and inequality:

I wouldn't even go out with them [Portuguese men]. I think that 'Canadianized' men have a lot more respect for the working woman and sharing household work.

Thus, in spite of her views on the use of violence to discipline children, as her parents did with her, Felicidade is repelled by the violence and abuse she describes as characteristic of many young, 'non-Canadianized' Portuguese men, including the spouses of some of her friends and her own brother, whom she describes as an alcoholic and verbally abusive.

The tension between Felicidade and her parents is not an unusual occurrence. What may be specific to the experience of Felicidade and other Portuguese children is the high level of parental strictness, including the use of physical abuse. Unlike Helena, Felicidade eventually reconciled with her parents, after twice running away from home, and returned to live with them when she was twenty-seven years old, until her marriage to her fiancé, David.

Both Felicidade and her mother criticize the education system for not measuring up to their expectations. This is a common theme in the case studies and in the broader Portuguese population in Toronto (see Chapter 5). Both Januaria and Suzana wanted a better education for their children than they themselves were able to achieve. This challenges the stereotype that Portuguese parents want their children leave school and enter the workforce as quickly as possible. Despite the difficulties posed to Portuguese by the Toronto educational system, most young Portuguese women – to a greater degree than men – seem to achieve some success, though not as high on average as the general Toronto population. Felicidade has been more successful than her brother, who has the added burden of alcoholism, and Helena also has managed to achieve a successful and satisfying career.

Both Helena and Felicidade chose partners from outside the Portuguese community. Both see this choice as a rejection of a *machismo* that does not fit with the more equitable visions of gender relations to which, as second-generation Portuguese women, they aspire.

Households, Identities, and Boundaries

Many authors writing on migration raise issues of women's 'boundedness' and lack of mobility. Trinh Minh-ha views women in general as traditionally restrained in their mobility, and therefore in their ability to leave home, except out of economic necessity. She describes a 'male economy of movement,' and women's lack of mobility due to their 'naturalized image ... as guardians of tradition, keepers of home and bearers of language' (Trinh Minh-ha 1994:15). De Pina Cabral describes an ideology which binds Portuguese women to their *terra*, just as they are bound to their household, while men are more mobile, able to leave the land and migrate (1984:90).[4] Belmira, a Portuguese homeworker in Toronto, describes how her attachment to her household is related to her experience in the Azores:

> I already came from Portugal like this, not liking to get out of the house. I only went out when I really needed to. And here it was difficult too because I wasn't used to working outside of the home. I learned to do all the work at home but with my mother ... When I came here I was obliged to go and work outside, and it was extremely difficult, and added to other hardships I went through. (Belmira, first-generation, garment homeworker, Azores)

The act of migration, and the fact that many Portuguese women migrate alone and set up households on their own, challenges both the notion that women are limited or tied to their homes, and the narrow definition of household boundaries.

Gender relations in first-generation Portuguese migrant/immigrant households are influenced by traditional ideologies and remembered attachments to home and households in Portugal. In the Canadian context of dichotomized public and private spaces, these are ideologies women have had to resist in order to claim a place in the wage workplace.

In Canada, the state reinforces naturalized images of women, arguing that it is the home (country of origin) culture that prevents immigrant/migrant women from moving out of the home (in Canada) to better jobs, more education, and language fluency. Canadian state multiculturalism privatizes women's lives, isolating them from the sense of the community espoused in multicultural discourse. Lack of access to language and job training is the result of a Canadian state multicultural policy that keeps many women dependent on others in their households.

Many second-generation women, through their critique of traditional gender role stereotyping in the household in Canada, resist the imposition of the traditions of their parents. They also criticize unequal gender ideologies that permeate immigration rules and regulations and define the boundaries of appropriate roles for women in a variety of spaces, including the household. Second-generation Portuguese women are challenging the politics which limit access to education and training for themselves and their children, seeking broader choices in employment than first-generation women, and arguing for the acceptance of difference inside and outside the Portuguese community on issues of sexuality, including choice of sexual partners, sexual identity, and definitions of family. First- and second-generation women, in their struggle to redefine the boundaries of Portuguese identity and home, seek to change their lives beyond the home and beyond the Portuguese community. Aspects of this struggle are explored in the next chapter.

Chapter Four

Working Lives

The working lives of Portuguese women in paid employment form a complex and multi-layered story which encompasses the many aspects of their identities as Canadian and/or Portuguese, as members of a particular class, and as mothers, wives, daughters, activists, and students. We now move our focus outward to the paid workplace and employment politics of Portuguese women in Toronto. It is in paid workplaces that the more ruthless aspects of Canadian state policy concerning immigration and ethnic identity are most keenly felt. As we focus on the everyday working lives of these women, the effects of Canadian state immigration and multicultural policies become clearer.

Canada's immigration policy refers explicitly to managing populations 'as informally and expeditiously as circumstances and fairness permit' (Gazette 1992:50). Expressions such as 'efficient,' 'fair' and 'expeditious' are used repeatedly by the government to describe immigration policy and its impact (Gazette 1992). These words, and the state policies in which they are embedded, are not separate from multicultural discourse in Canada, but are intertwined and interdependent with it. Overlaid with a democratic veneer of pluralism, immigration policy and legislation are contradictory: Although immigrant/migrant labour is desired, the persons in whom it is embodied are not (Kearney 1991). In other words, immigration policy, which ostensibly has been developed in order to regulate the entry of foreign workers, is concerned with separating 'labor from the jural person in which it is embodied' (ibid. 58). The 1998 federal Immigration Legislative Review document, *Not Just Numbers: A Canadian Framework for Future Immigration* (Immigration Legislative Review Advisory Group 1997), exemplifies this kind of discourse in its definition of workers as 'human capital,' not persons.

The discourse of globalization in this document confirms the hegemony of capitalism, extols its benefits, denies its weaknesses, and supports efforts to join its bandwagon. Canada's employment needs are contextualized as part of 'a global economy [that] has altered the nature of demand for human capital ...' (1998: 6.1). In fact, globalization has resulted in massive closures of manufacturing and industrial firms and concomitant job losses, which have accelerated the informalization of work in Toronto (Giles and Preston 1996:147). Multicultural discourse and policy disguise the raw edge of immigration policy by drawing attention away from the notion of immigrants as labour power, to define them as belonging to particular ethnic groups but not specific classes, genders, or racialized groups of workers. Ethnicity is a two-edged sword: On the one hand, ethnicity/ethnic identity is absorbed into state multicultural discourses and used to limit and control 'ethnics'; on the other hand, defining oneself as Portuguese may be a form of resistance to the oppressive practices of global capitalism.

This chapter examines two sides of the migration story: the attractiveness of low-paid immigrant labour power to Canadian employers, as opposed to the dreams, desires, and ambitions of immigrants for themselves, their families, and their communities. This juxtaposition mirrors definitions of the transnational migrant worker as both 'embodied capital' (human labour) and 'symbolic capital' (ethnic identity/ethnicity/collective identity) (Kearney 1991:63). Kearney argues that the creation of symbolic capital is part of a strategy of resistance on the part of the worker who desires to be more than 'foreign labour' or a disenfranchised worker, but also to be a human being who is part of a collective or a community, i.e., 'the Portuguese community.' This is precisely the problem with the formulation of state immigration policy: immigrant labour as a commodity is 'embodied in persons and persons with national identities ...' (ibid.: 58).

This chapter begins by using employment data to explore the extent to which Portuguese immigrant women have been part of a low-paid workforce in Canada and compares their situation to that of their daughters. This is followed by the case study of Rosa, who tells the story of her paid workplace and also the ways in which she has challenged inequality and built a better life. These two sides of the migration story are explored further in case studies of two strikes by cleaners and garment factory workers that graphically illustrate the type of labour force attachment and working conditions of 'human capital,' and the resistence of Portuguese immigrant women, in their efforts to build more equitable paid work relations. Migration has been success-ful for these women, insofar as their daughters now benefit from better education and working conditions than their mothers, despite the rac-ism they experienced in school and in paid workplaces. However, the costs of these struggles and successes to the Portuguese household and family have been high, as many of the women have indicated. Changes in the second generation are explored in the data below and in the latter part of the chapter.

Jobs across Generations

The working conditions of first-generation women demonstrate how immigrant women become 'human capital,' as defined in Canada's immigration policy. Although more Portuguese immigrant women than men of working age (20–64 years old) entered Canada during the height of the Portuguese immigration, this fact has not emerged in analyses of the Portuguese migration to Canada (see Figure 2.4). The first-genera-tion women who were interviewed worked mainly in two industries, manufacturing and other services (paid domestic work) (see Figure 4.1), and in a range of jobs in these industries (see Appendix A).

Canadian data indicate that in 1991, at the time this research was being carried out, the majority of Portuguese foreign-born women[1] worked in manufacturing (27%); other services, which include domes-tic service work (16%); the retail trade (13%); and health and social services (10%) (see Table 4.1). The most notable change for this group of women was a 10 per cent decrease from 1981 to 1991 in the numbers of women in manufacturing. Although the percentage of all other foreign-born women located in manufacturing has been considerably lower than that of Portuguese foreign-born, during the same period, there was also a 6 per cent decrease in the number of these women in manufacturing. This job loss was a direct result of the drastic restructur-ing that occurred in this industry during the 1980s. The numbers of Portuguese and of all other foreign-born women employed by this sector continued to decrease, as is demonstrated by the figures for 1996 (see Table 4.1).

The other major employer of Portuguese-born women has been 'other services,' a category that includes domestic service work. The steady increase in the numbers of Portuguese women in this category over the period of 1981–96 is a direct result of the loss of jobs in manufacturing. It is notable that the percentage of Portuguese-born women in this

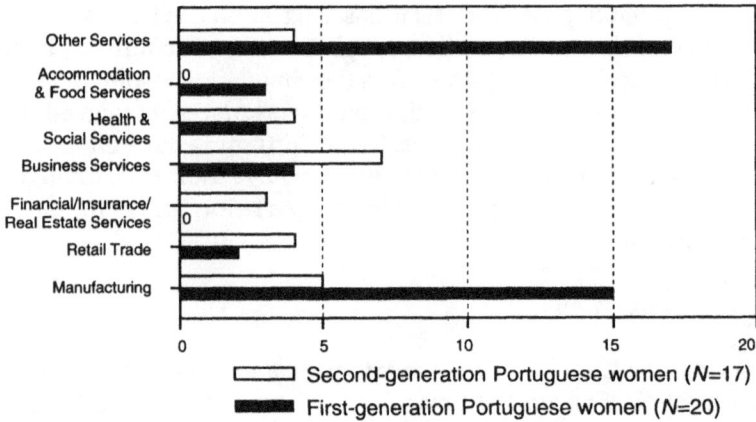

*Note: Some women (particularly first-generation women) had worked in two or more industries at the time of the interview. Thus, the numbers associated with each industry are not equivalent to the number of women interviewed. Appendix A describes all the jobs in which women were engaged.

Figure 4.1. Range and Variety of Industries: Two Generations of Portuguese Women Interviewed*

industry generally has been closer to that of Portuguese Canadian-born women than to the percentage of all other foreign-born women. These numbers confirm my finding that some second-generation Portuguese women – particularly those with less than high school graduation – still are located in this industry. Some of this group of women use domestic service jobs as a means of supporting themselves while they acquire other education and skills.

The second-generation women who were interviewed were distributed more evenly than first-generation women across business, retail trade, financial, health, and social service industries, as well as manufacturing and other services (see Figure 4.1). As a group, second-generation women have held a variety of jobs in these industries (see Appendix A), but as individuals, they have not changed jobs as frequently as their mothers, or as frequently as other Canadian-born women of similar ages (see Chapter Five). Furthermore, the tendency among second-generation women has not been to hold two or more jobs simultaneously, as did their mothers.

In 1991, most Portuguese Canadian-born women[2] were located in the following industrial sectors: the retail trade (31%), accommodation and food services (13%), health and social services (10%), other services

TABLE 4.1

Women in Canada by Selected Industry and by Ethnic Origin[a] / Place of Birth (as a percentage within ethnic origin / place of birth), 1981–96

Industry[b]	Ethnic Origin / Place of Birth	1981[c] %	1986 %	1991 %	1996 %
Manufacturing	Portuguese Foreign-Born	37.30	34.00	27.20	26.90
	Portuguese Canadian-Born	17.90	8.40	6.00	10.70
	All Other Foreign-Born	19.00	18.10	12.80	11.90
	All Other Canadian-Born	11.40	10.00	8.40	7.70
	Total	13.00	11.60	9.60	8.90
Retail Trade	Portuguese Foreign-Born	9.30	11.30	13.10	10.50
	Portuguese Canadian-Born	14.30	26.10	31.30	23.00
	All Other Foreign-Born	13.40	13.50	14.40	13.20
	All Other Canadian-Born	15.60	15.40	15.00	14.40
	Total	15.10	15.00	14.80	14.10
Financial/	Portuguese Foreign-Born	7.30	9.20	8.70	9.20
Insurance/	Portuguese Canadian-Born	5.40	10.90	9.40	8.30
Real Estate	All Other Foreign-Born	7.90	7.60	7.20	6.70
Services	All Other Canadian-Born	7.70	7.50	7.70	7.10
	Total	7.70	7.50	7.60	7.00
Business	Portuguese Foreign-Born	2.20	3.20	3.70	4.30
Services	Portuguese Canadian-Born	5.40	5.00	8.50	6.00
	All Other Foreign-Born	4.50	5.20	5.30	6.20
	All Other Canadian-Born	4.30	4.80	5.70	6.50
	Total	4.30	4.80	5.60	6.40
Health and	Portuguese Foreign-Born	8.70	6.10	10.30	11.30
Social	Portuguese Canadian-Born	10.70	10.90	9.90	15.40
Services	All Other Foreign-Born	13.90	14.40	15.50	17.30
	All Other Canadian-Born	14.60	14.60	15.70	16.90
	Total	14.40	14.50	15.60	17.00
Accommodation	Portuguese Foreign-Born	8.70	6.60	7.30	6.20
& Food	Portuguese Canadian-Born	8.90	16.00	13.40	12.70
Services	All Other Foreign-Born	8.90	8.90	9.00	9.30
	All Other Canadian-Born	9.50	9.40	9.00	9.20
	Total	9.40	9.30	9.00	9.30
Other	Portuguese Foreign-Born	13.46	14.60	16.00	17.50
Services	Portuguese Canadian-Born	10.71	10.10	9.70	11.40
	All Other Foreign-Born	7.35	9.20	9.70	10.30
	All Other Canadian-Born	6.56	8.60	8.30	9.30
	Total	6.76	8.80	8.70	9.60

Notes:

a. Only those reporting Portuguese as a single response are included in the Portuguese ethnic group.

b. According to 1980 Statistics Canada SIC Major Groups

c. The category 'Other Services' for 1981 is an approximation of the industries included in 'Other Services' for 1986–96.

Source: Based on a 2–3% sample of the Canadian population in Statistics Canada, Public Use Sample Tapes (1981) and Public Use Microdata Files (1986, 1991, 1996)

(10%), financial/insurance/real estate services (9%), and business services (9%) (see Table 4.1). Significantly, the percentage of Portuguese Canadian-born women in the retail trade in 1991 was twice that of all other Canadian-born women, and this figure more than doubled for Portuguese Canadian-born women in the decade from 1981–91, before falling off by 8 per cent in 1996. Another set of data reveals the fluctuation in the number of Portuguese Canadian-born women in manufacturing: 18 per cent in 1981, dropping to 6 per cent in 1991 (at least partly due to restructuring), and then increasing to 11 per cent in 1996.

Although many Portuguese-born women work at two or more types of jobs simultaneously, Statistics Canada data contain information for only one of the jobs at any one time. Qualitative data give a much expanded portrait of the working lives of both generations. Portuguese immigrant women came to Canada to make a better life for themselves and their children, and despite the inequality they have experienced, most have succeeded, as exemplified by the story of Rosa that follows.

A Better Life

Rosa, a First-Generation Woman

As a girl growing up in Lisbon, Rosa's dream was to become a hairdresser. But Rosa's mother was adamant about not letting her pursue this profession because she thought that hairdressers were all 'whorish.' Instead, she encouraged Rosa to acquire the more respectable skills of a seamstress:

> And you know in those times, our mothers used to tell us that we should learn sewing. So against my will, that's what I did. I finished my elementary school when I was twelve and then I went to learn to be an apprentice dressmaker. At the beginning, of course, you didn't learn anything, you just picked up pins and were an errand girl. And then around fourteen years of age, I went into this company where I stayed until after my son was born. And I liked it very much because I used to like the decoration part of the work.

Rosa married at seventeen. When her husband completed his military service, after 25 April 1974, the family migrated to Canada.[3] Six months after Rosa arrived in Canada, her sister-in-law found her a job in a plastic bottle factory in Toronto. She couldn't speak English in

TABLE 4.2
Rosa's Work History

Year	Year	Year	
1953	Born (Lisbon)	1975	Migrates to Canada with husband and son, Luís
1954	2	1976	Begins works in bottle factory
1955	3	1977	25
1956	4	1978	26
1957	5	1979	27
1958	6	1980	Joins Portuguese Canadian Democratic Association and Portuguese theatre group
1959	7	1981	29
1960	Starts school		
1961	9		
1962	10	1982	30
1963	11	1983	31
1964	Leaves school and becomes apprentice dressmaker	1984	Work injury; leaves factory and goes on Workers Compensation
1965	13	1985	33
1966	Begins to work as an interior decorator	1986	Begins working at cloakroom in athletic centre
1967	15	1987	35
1968	16	1988	Buys house in Toronto
1969	Marries	1989	37
1970	18	1990	Begins working at snack bar in athletic centre; also cleans athletic equipment and houses part-time
1971	Son Luís is born; stops paid work	1991	39
1972	20	1992	40
1973	21		
1974	22		

those days, and because she worked with other Portuguese women in the factory, she didn't learn to speak English there and still doesn't. Even though she 'earned good money,' she was taken aback at the realization that she would have to pay for childcare in Canada, which she found expensive. By doing shift work and catching a few hours sleep here and there, she was able to share childcare with her husband:

When I got home in the morning he [her husband] would have left just a bit before and I kept awake until around eight when I could wash my son, dress him, and take him to school. And then I'd sleep a bit until eleven and I'd get up to go and get him for lunch. And then I'd take him to school, come back and go back to bed and then have to get up at three and go get him again.

It was a struggle for Rosa and her husband to care for their family and personal needs and also to show up at their factories ready to work. She sometimes felt that her own life was of no interest to her employer. She raised questions about the strength of the union at the bottle factory to address these issues:

In the factory it was like this – we used to talk a lot that we'd go on strike, we'd vote but once we got there [to the union meeting], everybody would keep their mouth shut. They'd approve everything.

Most of the workers could not understand the proceedings of these meetings, since they were held in English. Rosa concluded that it was a company union:

The union was not that much on the side of the workers. They also knew that the people couldn't speak English and couldn't defend themselves. Those meetings, they were in English and we couldn't understand a thing.

Lacking the cohesion of a union, the workers thus became divided among themselves:

In our group of three, working at the machine, the third woman, who didn't ally herself with us, spoke good English. She was Azorean. But she'd make fun of the others. If we'd ask her to translate a question for us she'd laugh and say that the question was useless. Perhaps for her it was, but not for us.

After eight years at the factory, Rosa had an accident, quit her job, and went on worker's compensation for two years. When she could work again, she found a job in an athletic club, first working in the cloakroom and then cooking and serving food in the snack bar. Although she says she likes this job – she enjoys cooking and she feels that serving people has helped to improve her English skills – it is full of contradictions for her:

> Well it's the kind of work where you see people. You socialize a bit.
> However, it's people that I have nothing in common with. They are very
> rich and it revolts me to have to serve people like that. But what can I do?
> It's my job, my bread and butter. I thought it was a good idea because then
> I would have the possibility of learning some English, because I never
> went to school here.

Rosa talks about the inequality in her workplace, where the men
make more than the women. She would like to challenge her employer,
but was unsuccessful in getting her co-worker to join her:

> I always work with a Greek woman. The others change each summer. I
> don't have any problem at all with her. However, we could do more
> together if she was a different kind of person. But she's sixty years old, she
> doesn't give a damn anymore. The men make more money than us. I
> know that one of the men makes $13.00 an hour and the other $10.00, and
> I make $8.60. It's very low. So I think if we got together we could do
> something. Because to begin with, if we do the same work, we can't have
> different wages. It's a great discrimination.

When she approached the club owners about the discrimination in
pay, Rosa was praised for the improvements she had made in the snack
food service, but was told that the pay scale was not the responsibility
of the club owners or members. She was told she should go to a 'labour
department' to argue for more money:

> There are many [club members] who like me, so I take advantage and this
> is how you have to do it, of course. And they tell me, 'Rosa, it is so good
> that you work in the snack bar because you changed certain things for the
> better.' So I took advantage of this and I said, 'Well, they pay more to those
> who don't deserve it.' And she said, 'What? You earn less than Ken?' 'Sure,
> he makes $13.00 and I make $8.60.' She told me, 'Oh, yeah? So you should
> go to the labour department and make a complaint.' And she is a member.
> She is one of the club owners.

One of the more outrageous and telling experiences about worker-
employer-client relations that Rosa describes concerns the 'friendship'
extended by some of the club members. The fact that one of these

members was able to relate to Rosa only in her role as a cleaner or cook demonstrates the impermeability of class boundaries:

> I have certain members there who really liked me. For example, when I worked in the cloak room, they'd come up and ask me, 'Don't you have a free day to go and clean my house?' There is one of them that I got closer to and I told her, 'Well, why don't you ever invite me to go for supper at your place? The only thing you ask me is to go and clean your house.' And she told me, 'Well, I thought about that. One day, I'll invite you, and you'll cook, and I'll pay everything. I'll have a person to clean up after you, or I'll clean it myself.'

Rosa belies the stereotype of the passive Portuguese immigrant woman. She would like another type of job, mostly because of 'the way they [the club members/owners] talk down to you.' But she also resists a subservient relationship, by turning the tables: 'If they don't talk well to me, they won't get as well served.' Rosa's expression of revulsion for the wealthy clients that she serves, her friendliness with some of these same clients, and her acknowledgment that she has taken advantage of her contact with them to advance her personal situation, express simultaneously class consciousness, pragmatism, and some quality of human contact that is beyond class analysis. There is a dynamism to possessing a working-class consciousness, while engaging, in a variety of ways, with people of other classes. This is exemplified also in Rosa's remarks about her son's experiences in school:

> He'd say things like, 'We have to keep a certain distance. Even if we don't have anything, we have to look as if we have a strong personality.' And I'd tell him, 'Son, sometimes I think you pretend that you're rich.' And he said, 'Well, mum, I'm taking my best clothes to school. That's what I see around me, and that's what I have to do.' [4]

Although buying a house was a strategic investment for Rosa and her husband, as it is for many Portuguese in Toronto, this decision also addressed the class discrimination that Luís felt at school. Her description of her son Luís's experience in school stretches traditional definitions of class. House ownership and clothing are the symbols of class status for the students:

> We bought a house three years ago. It was an investment – we figured

we'd be paying the same amount of money if we bought a house [as renting an apartment]. I also thought that Luís felt bad that we didn't own a house. He'd tell me for example, 'We've been here for so many years, how come we don't have a house yet?' He went to a school where many people from High Park went, people with money. And he heard people talking about it. He'd tell us, 'The others have worked less than you and yet they own a house.' He also told us that he noticed a certain discrimination against kids who didn't own a home.

Like other immigrant women, Rosa does several 'part times,' jobs to maintain her household through periods when her husband is laid off, as well as to have 'money for extras' for Luís and for occasional travel to Portugal. These jobs, which have included washing sports equipment for the athletic club as well as cleaning houses, have given Rosa more independence, particularly because this money does not always go to household essentials, as her salary from the athletic club does:

When I picked up these part times, I felt I wanted to have money for extras. My money is my own. With my salary, my cheque, I buy things for home. That money, I can't save any of it. My husband's wages go to the bank and go towards the mortgage and for utilities. Whereas mine, I do shopping with it and then I save the rest. It's still ours of course, but I'm the one who controls the money.

A spirit of pride in her ability to work and bring in a pay cheque is reflected in Rosa's attitude about housework in her own household, where she maintains a sense of autonomy and independence:

I consider myself to be fulfilled because I have my work, I'm independent. Perhaps I wouldn't feel this way if I was a sick woman and I couldn't move about or work. But I'm a normal person. I come home from work and if I want to do housework, I do. If I don't, then I don't. I hear women say, 'Well, women are etc., etc.' But I only do things if I want to. You know, I've got to get home with my husband. I cook supper. If I want to clean up the kitchen, I do. If I don't, I won't. Nobody forces me to do anything.

Rosa is quite clear about her own class identity:

I'm working-class. Immigration hasn't changed that. There [in Portugal] I worked, here I work. Here I have a house, but it's not paid. It could have been the same thing there. So nothing has changed. I don't have a hard life. I work, I have my wages; my husband works, he has his wages, so far. Fortunately, I've never been through any hardship, whereas I have friends who have been through very difficult times and I've helped them. I've never lost my job.

Rosa's reflection that her life would likely have been the same in Portugal, had she stayed there (i.e., as a working-class woman confronting many of the same economic issues), brings to mind Bannerji's words: 'The emigre condition is in no way better or worse than living at "home" within nation states.' (1995:186). Oppressed from her early years in Portugal – where the job that she really wanted was considered 'whorish' – to her life in Canada, where childcare costs are exorbitant, the union in the factory where she works unhelpful, and the athletic club pays her less than the men, Rosa nevertheless says that, as a women and a political activist, she would never be able to do in Portugal what she does in Canada. She refers to her involvement in the Portuguese Democratic Association and the politics of the theatre group in which she acts. From these two related communities, she draws political strength and an identity of resistance that spills over into her working and family life. She says:

> I always belonged to the Cultural Committee and the Kitchen Committee of the Portuguese Democratic Association. Saturdays and Sundays we serve supper. I'm there in the kitchen once a month. The Theatre Group does not belong to the Association. Although I, and the other people too, feel that any time we are on stage we are really representing the Democratic Association. Well, I think it has helped me and the other women because I know that in Portugal I would never be able to do what I am doing here. But it depends where you lived [in Portugal]. Especially in the area, that I lived, you didn't see any women involved in anything.

Struggles and Successes in the Workplace

The significance of the resistance by Portuguese first-generation women to exploitative working conditions cannot be underestimated, since these struggles are also a critique of immigration policy in Canada, which has oppressed women in quite specific and harsh ways. In the following two cases of strikes against a cleaning company and in a factory, two unionized Portuguese immigrant women, Lurdes and

Idalina, describe their efforts to improve their working conditions, using the strength of the unions in their struggles. Lurdes is from the Azores and has worked in several different kinds of jobs, in services and manufacturing. Idalina is from Madeira and had worked only in manufacturing at the time of the interview. The strike against the cleaning company, which occurred in the mid-1970s, involved mainly Portuguese women, most of whom could not speak English. Despite this they managed to acquire enough information and courage to support one another through what was for many a traumatic experience. The strike in the sock factory occurred in the autumn of 1987 and lasted seven weeks, during which some of the workers broke ranks and went back to work. It was a bitter protest for better pay and working conditions in the factory, and included a boycott of the company's socks by Christmas shoppers. The final settlement included a minimal pay increase, a longer contract, and an overall improvement to benefits. Workers claimed these concessions indicated a greater respect by the employer and represented a significant achievement by the workers.

Office Cleaners

> There was a strike with the cleaners because of dirty garbage bags. It turned out to be a serious problem because no one could speak English. Only me and another lady knew how to speak a bit of English. My English was worse than it is today. I was a steward for the union. I said, I don't know how to do this job because I never worked in a place with the unions, but I went anyway. The union man, Mr. Jordan, liked me right away, to have someone who could speak some English. That's why he asked me to be the steward.
>
> Our bosses were giving us dirty garbage bags that had been emptied, to use again. But they stank, and some pregnant women used to throw up when they opened the bags. It was a terrible situation, so we had a meeting with the union. Some ladies took the bags for the union people to smell. They called Mr. Dan Heap who at that point was working for the unions. He smelt the bags too, and he found it impossible that human beings should be working in those conditions.
>
> We started a strike on a Friday evening. The ladies went to tell the forelady that they wouldn't come to work and she called the big boss. He brought a little hand-held tape recorder, and I'd never seen anything like that. I was chosen to speak because of my English. Every time he would ask me questions and I would answer he would tape my answers. I'm not

the kind of person who loses my head and swears. I only said that we'd only go to work if they gave us clean bags. He said he wouldn't. Then he told us that we should all take off our uniforms and go home. We said, 'We won't go home, because we have a union and we have our bills to pay.' He called a Portuguese man who was an assistant manager – a Portuguese man from the Island of Terceira – to come and talk to us and send us home. I put my hand on his chest and I told him [the man from Terceira], 'We have a union and you don't. Let your people speak and defend themselves.' So he left and I never saw him again.

We didn't go home, so he told us that he was going to call the police. In the meantime, the other lady who could also speak some Portuguese, called the union for them to come over. Mr. Jordan and Dan Heap came. Six police – enormous police – came in. When they arrived the manager told them, 'Take this woman out of this building as soon as you can.' I still get goose bumps when I recount this. They asked him, 'Why do you want us to remove her from here?' The manager said, 'Because she doesn't want to work.' The police didn't even talk to me and they asked him, 'What's the reason?' And he said, 'Because the bags were dirty.' So he turned to me and said, 'Do you want to go to work or not?' And I said, 'Yes, we want to go to work but we want clean bags.' The police told the boss, 'Could we see you in the office for a minute?' The police never talked to me.

Then he called for me and another three women from the union. I went in – I was so nervous that I wept. I was the only one who talked. I told them if he didn't feel sorry for the poor Portuguese women that worked so hard that he should try to do the same cleaning job employing Canadians and he would see how much more money he'd spend. So we won, because on Monday we went to work on a contract for clean bags. The women were so happy that they lifted me up in the air. They said that I was the one that had solved the problem.

Five women had gone to work during this strike. The others wanted to wait for them outside of the building and strip them naked as punishment – beat them up. I told them that they shouldn't do that because those women did not understand the problem. I said, 'Let's go home – if we have bills to pay, they also have bills to pay.' I came home to sleep but I couldn't sleep a wink. Even today I shudder to think. I cried so much; I was so nervous. But the following day so many people called me in support. They told me, 'Mrs. D., go to work – don't quit. If on Monday they don't treat you well, you tell us. But please go back on Monday.' I went, and in reality nobody mistreated me. But other ladies who were very friendly with the *bossa* would tell me to my face, 'Oh, I just think about the union when I go to the toilet.' They were mocking us of course but one of these woman was punished sometime later – she was fired because she was stealing from the company. Whereas I left when I wanted.

There were perhaps over a hundred women and they were all on my side. Out of those – over a hundred – only five went to work against our will. And I think they were probably sorry afterwards, because they worked the whole night overtime to clean the whole building – Saturday and Sunday as well. We had lots of threats, but in the end it worked out well. I think it is a good thing to have a union. I still meet ladies who work there – they all know me but I don't know all of them, of course. But when they see me, they hug me and say, 'She was our mother!' The immigrant woman is very afraid to speak up, because she can't talk English and becomes very frightened.' (Lurdes, cleaner, first-generation, Azores)

Factory Workers

Before the strike they used to treat workers in a different way. They didn't exactly beat them, but they didn't treat them well either. They didn't know the people's names and they used to call them by numbers ... like prisoners in a prison. Nowadays treatment is somewhat better due to the strike we had. Actually, even before the union group got in there, they used to give raises to some people and not to others. If they liked somebody, they would give her 20 cents extra an hour and if they didn't, they would only give them 5 cents. They abused the workers, so the union came in and things improved, but they continued to take advantage of workers and use them as slaves. And so some people filed grievances with the union, and the union figured that things weren't going well. So the union committee decided to go on strike; we were on strike for almost two months. Some people who had originally voted for the strike ... after a week or three weeks, they went back to work to please the bosses. But those who had human love [solidarity], they stuck to their guns and stayed on strike. So nowadays they don't abuse workers like they used to.

I'm not sure how many people work there. I'd say over three hundred people. Nowadays I don't know, perhaps more people because they have three shifts and they also have a warehouse. I work on the first shift which is from 7:00 a.m. to 4:30 p.m. Most are Portuguese from the Azores, but for me they are all the same. I get along with everybody. Yes, some are two-faced; they speak well to you and then they stab you in the back. The *bossa* was a Portuguese woman and she was a bitch. Instead of siding with people from her own nationality, she was even harsher with them. She's lost her job and we have an Italian man and we don't have anything to complain about him. We do our work; he smiles at us; he greets us, whereas the Portuguese woman knew only to say negative things. So we are fine now with our foreman. On top of him, higher, is the owner, who is Jewish. When he wants to be nice and kind, he is, but when he isn't, he just turns his back on us. But it's not like certain places I've heard about where people say, 'Well, I don't know who my boss is, who the owner is.' I don't have that problem. I know my owner, the father; I know the son; I know the family.

I participated in the strike; I did everything. It was cold because it took place during the wintertime. But we had barbecues. There were some oil bins, and we used to warm ourselves up by burning wood in them. We sang; we danced. Of course, we were hoping for a decision to be made by the bosses concerning the contract. We enjoyed ourselves too. The saddest thing, of course, were those workers who initially voted for the strike and supported us but then betrayed us. That was the reason why we lost. And that's why the strike lasted so long. Most women went back. So that when they saw that they had most of them on their side, they turned against the women on strike. We got strike pay but, of course, the union paid us very little ... couldn't compare to our regular wages. Some didn't have the means to stay on strike; they had mortgages to pay; they had to pay the babysitter. Others found other jobs while they were on strike. Only the faithful ones stayed until the very end and the group was growing smaller.

So the labour boards in the end sided with the bosses and forced us to go back to work. We got very little. We got a three-year contract, whereas before we had a two-year contract. They gave us 35 cents raise per hour. Very few benefits. After the strike, they gave us a bit more on our benefits. Most accepted it. And also due to the cost of living and inflation and whatever you call it. Of course before they used to pay OHIP and now it's government that pays. They gave us a bit more for our dental plan and other things, I can't remember right now. We can't say it's very bad. They treat people better; they call them by their names; they are more diplomatic. Before they used to come up to you and say, 'Do this!' And if we protested they'd say, 'Do it right now.' Nowadays they will say, 'Please will you do this? Can you do this for me? If you could do it now, I'd thank you.' And of course this is good for morale. We're not slaves.

The factory is going to move to the West Mall in Etobicoke. They thought that the area that they are in now near the SkyDome would be reserved for the Olympic Games and would be very expensive. They were going to sell the building to make hotels. So they decided to rent a building in West Mall. The son of the boss told us that, if possible, they would try not to move too far or not to move to the States because he liked his employees, because we are part of the family. So he is going to make an effort to take all of the present employees to West Mall.' (Idalina, factory worker, first-generation, Madeira)

Divisions and Solidarities in the Workplace

These stories demonstrate the attitude of Portuguese women toward their employers, whom they fear, but also recognize as exploiting their labour and the labour of other immigrant women. The cleaners' strike in particular shows how a lack of language skills is related to exploitation in the workplace, fear of demanding basic health and safety rights, and a diminished sense of self-respect. In the factory, the paternalism of factory owners creates contradictions for Portuguese women workers, who see themselves as exploited and overworked, but as part of a factory 'family.'[5] The struggles of the women to gain respect as workers and to have their work regarded as valuable and important are central to an understanding of class as a process, rather than a static structure. These examples of the way in which classes are formed 'in struggle' (Thompson 1963; Laclau 1977) demonstrate how the everyday working and living experiences of women are shaped by the gendered multicultural, immigration, and citizenship practices of Canada. On the one hand, state practices have limited the development of collective struggles across various minority groups with members of the indigenous working class by defining immigrants as members of ethnic groups rather than as workers. On the other hand, these same practices form the basis of the exploitation of immigrants in the paid workplace.

Portuguese regional differences (Azores versus mainland Portugal), which the women describe as having significant importance outside the workplace (i.e., in community and inter-family relationships), are raised in contradictory ways by Portuguese women in the paid workplace. A desire for solidarity in opposition to the employer was expressed by some women. Worker-manager/employer relations are foregrounded as problematic:

You know, they often say that there is a problem between mainlanders and Azoreans. I never had that. We were perhaps over four hundred Portuguese women, mostly Azoreans. And the rest of us were from the mainland, very few from the mainland. And there was never a problem such as saying, 'Well, that's because you're from the Azores or you're from the mainland.' I've heard many people complain about that. But I never had that problem. We used to help each other. (Laurinda, first-generation, factory worker, private cleaner, mainland)

However, regional differences are highlighted when they overlap with workplace hierarchies. In most cases, the women's Portuguese *bossas* (forewomen) were criticized and mistrusted, particularly when there was a regional difference. They described how favoured treatment is bestowed arbitrarily, as well as how it is institutionalized into a hierarchical system:

The *bossa* was a very difficult woman. She was Portuguese from the mainland. She thought she'd make me break down and cry because there were several people that she made cry every day. But I told her, 'I'm sorry, but you'll never see me cry.' (Januaria, first-generation, cleaner, Azores)

As described in the two cases of strikes above, as well as in Rosa's case study, hierarchical power relations are strengthened by workers' inability to communicate in English. One defiant worker said her lack of English language skills left her with a sense of powerlessness:

Of course we know that what the *bossas* say comes from the manager. The manager is the worst. It's the lowest you can find. She's [the *bossa*] double-faced. She screws you up behind your back and that's no good. [But] she has no manners speaking with people. What she says in English to her boss is very different than what she says to me in Portuguese. So I can only defend myself when she is speaking to me in Portuguese. (Ilda, first-generation, cleaner, mainland Portugal)

Although their lack of English skills prevented them from becoming active union representatives, it did not prevent them from defending their own and their co-workers' rights against the *bossas*. Nor did their inability to communicate in English prevent them from acquiring information about deteriorating working conditions. The lack of access to English language classes has left these women more vulnerable to workplace abuse and diminished their knowledge of the factors involved in their own exploitation, but it has not extinguished their spirit of struggle.[6]

First-generation Portuguese immigrant women in Toronto have confronted and fought against highly exploitative working conditions in cleaning and factory jobs. They have mixed feelings about their lives in Canada and, in most cases, do not view it as 'the land of opportunity' to which they initially believed they were coming. Their struggles in the workplace are linked to this knowledge of another life and certainly of another vision of what they thought migration would bring. Yet these women recognize that work in Canada has brought a degree of material wealth that they could not acquire in Portugal, particularly if they have come from the Azores. In various ways, most state that the physical and emotional costs to themselves and their families have been too high. In the pages that follow, I explore some of the changes – positive and negative – in the second generation of women workers.

Into the Second Generation

Given an education, 'Canadian experience,' and fluency in English, the paid work experiences of the second-generation women are different from their mothers. Like their mothers, most of the second-generation women interviewed work in places where the majority of the workforce is women. However, they describe their jobs as different from their mothers' jobs in several ways. One recurring theme is that the jobs of second-generation women are 'clean':

> Theirs [her parents' jobs] are more labour-orientated, mine is more cleri-
> cal. And it's a cleaner job. They're involved in the cleaning industry and
> manual jobs and getting dirty, while I'm in an office atmosphere. (Julie,
> second-generation, air coordinator, travel agency, mainland Portugal)

Most second-generation women work in retail, clerical, administrative, and related occupations, and most are non-unionized. As well, few of these women have experienced either the extreme effects of the disruption caused by immigration to Canada or the consequences of being unable to communicate in English. Their workplace concerns often have to do with equity issues that they consciously identify as discrimination against women and the Portuguese. Eunice's ambitions for a senior management position challenge the status quo at the bank in which she works. She is concerned about gender equity:

> The one thing that bothers me is the fact that the majority of senior
> management individuals are men. Yet those of us in middle management,

the majority of whom are females, we seem to do all the work and run the fort. Yet, they get all the credit. I find that's one thing that peeves me to no end. (Eunice, second-generation, accounting officer in bank, Azores)

Unlike many of their mothers, they sometimes feel powerless to challenge these injustices:

I think we all understand the problems, but not all of us know what to do. (Rosa, second-generation, community worker, Azores)

I find people more unified in Portugal than here. Banks aren't unionized [in Canada], they do whatever they want with us. I guess banking is the worst place because they can do whatever they really want. Management has to work forty hours. Non-management works thirty-seven and a half. And even if you work forty hours you're expected to stay longer if anything goes wrong. I don't know really what the union would bring. (Anna, second-generation, loans officer, bank, mainland Portugal)

Unlike their mothers, most second-generation women look to formal politics as a way of enacting change. They vote in elections, and some work for political parties. Class, ethnic, and gender identity have changed for second-generation Portuguese women. Most refer to themselves as middle class, while, in the majority of cases, they regard their parents as working class or of working-class origin. However, some second-generation women expressed caution in defining their class position:

Mid or low [class] ... I try so hard for what we have. It really depends. What you have is really not important. It's what you do to have it. I don't even go on holidays every year. There's so many things and if you do those things then you won't have other things that are important to you. So it's very hard to put yourself on a level. I guess you belong to what you really want to make believe that you really belong to. You've got to work, if you're in the low class. You've got to work. (Anna, second-generation, loans officer, bank, mainland)

Another second-generation woman described how her roots in the ethnic and class identity of her parents guided her life:

My lifestyle is very much middle class. I think there are very many Portuguese like me who have become middle class, who have come from working class, who have just developed a different lifestyle. But the working-class roots are still there ... For me, to have working-class roots means to have a consciousness. It means that I do things always remembering that side of my life. I have chosen to do things in my life a certain way because of that. (Rosa, second-generation, community worker, Azores)

It is difficult for women to organize collectively in many non-unionized jobs. However, even the women who were unionized were not well informed about their union. One second-generation woman described her union as a kind of discussion group, used to diffuse the frustrations of workers:

It's important to have a union. I think without a union, who do you turn to? Our union is composed of all of our staff. We sit down and have conversations with one another and try to help. If someone is having a problem in the workplace we try to meet the needs of that person ... I don't know what union it is that I belong to. We meet at one of the work areas here. (Emilia, second-generation, office manager, Azores)

Conclusion

Dangerous and oppressive working conditions are not unique to immigrant women. All immigrant workers confront the negative effects of immigration and multicultural state policies that disembody labour from the worker and define a person as an 'ethnic,' devoid of any identity as a worker. When immigrant workers are defined as labour and not as persons, or when multicultural discourse is used as a means to deflect discussions about the Portuguese person as a worker, even the very limited rights of citizenship that are accorded to immigrants are denied, as Amelia poignantly describes:

We are doing eight hours work within five hours. And yet we have to do it really well, because if we ask for help it's worse. What they don't understand is that extra effort comes off our bodies and our family life because we are ruining our health and we don't have any energy after we come home. (Amelia, cleaner, first-generation)

Rosa's work in the Portuguese Democratic Association and the Portuguese Theatre Group gives her a community of Portuguese with whom to share and explore a Portuguese identity and to question the inequalities she and the others confront as a community and as workers in Canada. Along with the household, these are sites in which symbolic forms of the reproduction of Portuguese identity are enacted and shared. They include working-class politics and a consciousness that spills into the household where Rosa challenges her son's desire to appear 'rich,' while at the same time trying to preserve his dignity.

The communities that Portuguese workers formed in both the cleaning and factory labour disputes extend the notion of symbolic capital beyond ethnic collectivities to other forms of resistance that potentially can link to broader 'internationalized and multi-focussed social movements' (Stasiulis and Bakan 1997:133). The next chapter pursues the theme of the relationship between nationalism and multiculturalism, challenging the notion that claims to a Portuguese identity can lead to more equitable access to resources for immigrants and their descendants, while critiquing the limited inroads to non-nationalist-based coalitions. In particular, I look at the example of access to education for Portuguese.

Appendix A. Paid Occupations: First- and Second-Generation Women

First Generation	Place of Birth	Age at Time of Interview	Industry in Canada	Type of Job	Income at Time of Interview
Amélia	Azores	38	Manufacturing	Factory work	Less than $12,000
Maria	Azores	44	Other Services Other Services	Office cleaning Office cleaning; domestic help in law firm	$12,000–20,000
Fátima	Azores	40	Manufacturing Other Services Accommodation and Food Services Retail trade Education Services	Soldering iron Cleaning laundromat Waitress Cashier Teaching assistant; interpreter in schools	Unknown
Conceição	Azores	63	Manufacturing	Wool weaver; making lamp shades; seamstress	$30,000–50,000 (from husband's worker's compensation)
Alda	Azores	36	Manufacturing	Seamstress: coats, curtains	$18,000
Lucy	Azores	47	Other Services Other Services Business Services, Educational Services; Health and Social Services Business Services	Office cleaner Office cleaner Photographer; teaching heritage classes; interpreter; community worker Receptionist	$25,000

Appendix A. Paid Occupations: First- and Second-Generation Women (Continued)

First Generation	Place of Birth	Age at Time of Interview	Industry in Canada	Type of Job	Income at Time of Interview
Lurdes	Azores	58	Other Services	Babysitter; office cleaner; house cleaner	unknown
Manuela	Azores	37	Manufacturing Manufacturing	Seamstress: men's ties Making jewellery; car parts	$20,000–30,000
Januária	Azores	39	Other Services Other Services Manufacturing	Hospital cleaner; nurse's aid Building cleaner Plant nursery worker; seamstress; chair maker; clothes presser	unknown
Vinnie	Madeira	32	Manufacturing Business Services	Making furniture; toys; hosiery/socks Union organizer	$12,000–20,000
Gina	Madeira	50	Other Services	House cleaner	$30,000
Idalina	Madeira	38	Manufacturing	Making purses; hosiery/socks	unknown
Suzana	Mainland	55	Other Services Other Services	Beautician Supervisor, building cleaners	unknown
Ilda	Mainland	40	Other Services	Building and house cleaner	$16,000
Clarisse	Mainland	42	Manufacturing Retail Trade	Making jewellery Store supervisor	$20,000–30,000

Appendix A. Paid Occupations: First- and Second-Generation Women *(Continued)*

First Generation	Place of Birth	Age at Time of Interview	Industry in Canada	Type of Job	Income at Time of Interview
Cora	Mainland	45	Other Services Health and Social Services; Business Services	Building cleaner Community worker; newspaper editor	$20,000
Tucha	Mainland	58	Manufacturing Other Services Accommodation and Food Services	Making glass; plastic flowers; seamstress Chambermaid Cafeteria worker	$10,000
Maria José	Mainland	44	Manufacturing Health and Social Services	Seamstress: curtains Hospital housekeeper and supervisor	$30,000–50,000
Rosa	Mainland	40	Manufacturing Other Services Accommodation and Food Services	Making plastic bottles House cleaner Food service worker	$12,000–20,000
Laurinda	Mainland	56	Manufacturing Other Services	Seamstress House cleaner	$12,000
Rosália	Mainland	51	Other Services Manufacturing	Chambermaid; building cleaner Making watch parts	unknown

Appendix A. Paid Occupations: First- and Second-Generation Women (*Continued*)

Second Generation	Place of Birth	Age at Time of Interview	Industry	Type of Job	Income at Time of Interview
Eunice	Toronto	23	Finance and Insurance	Teller, accounts payable	$20,000–30,000
Ricarda	Toronto	24	Manufacturing	Seamstress: hosiery/socks	$12,000–20,000
Anna	Mainland Portugal	32	Finance and Insurance	Bank worker	$30,000–50,000
Lidia	Mainland Portugal	29	Finance and Insurance	Trust company worker	$30,000–50,000
Rosie	Azores	39	Business Services	Receptionist	$30,000–50,000
Lucy	Azores	40	Business Services	Legal secretary	$12,000–20,000
Rosa	Azores	33	Health and Social Services	Community development officer	$20,000–30,000
Fernanda	Mainland Portugal	32	Health and Social Services	Community development officer; translator	$20,000–30,000
Emilia	Toronto	22	Business Services	Secretary; office coordinator	$20,000–30,000
Lucinda	Azores	31	Business Services	Secretary	$20,000–30,000
			Health and Social Services	Children's Aid worker	
Julie	Mainland Portugal	27	Retail Trade Business Services	Sales clerk	$20,000–30,000
				Travel agent	
Felicidade	Mainland Portugal	27	Retail Trade	Sales clerk	$20,000–30,000
			Business Services	Secretary	

Appendix A. Paid Occupations: First- and Second-Generation Women *(Concluded)*

Second Generation	Place of Birth	Age at Time of Interview	Industry	Type of Job	Income at Time of Interview
Christina	Azores	23	Other Services Retail Trade Manufacturing	Assistant to hairdresser Sales clerk Glass design; food processing	$12,000–19,000
Helena	Mainland Portugal	36	Other Services Manufacturing Manufacturing Business Services Health and Social Services	Building cleaner Factory Factory Secretary Community worker	$20,000–30,000
Filomena	Mainland Portugal	26	Other Services	House cleaner	$12,000–19,000
Irene	Azores	38	Other Services Manufacturing	Building cleaner; babysitter Car parts	$12,000–19,000
Antonia	Toronto	22	Retail Trade	Sales clerk	$12,000–19,000

Chapter Five

Ethnoculturalism, Education, and Restructuring

Nationalisms exist to protect and promote the interests of specific, usually ethnically defined groups. In the absence of alliances with labour unions, anti-racist and feminist organizations, or health and education coalitions, ethnicity intersects with class and becomes a dominant form of organization among many immigrant groups. In Canada, the ethnic nationalisms associated with immigrant groups are unlikely ever to develop into full-fledged nationalist struggles (i.e., involving military action and claims to territory in Canada).[1] In fact, most forms of ethnic nationalism are controlled and managed by a dominant class-based, Anglo-nationalism, expressed in Canadian state multiculturalist policies. Those basing their claims to more equitable access to education, health, and employment on a Portuguese ethnic identity will be successful only to the extent conceded by multiculturalism, which in the Canadian liberal capitalist state always serves the needs of its dominant group first. Most immigrant groups to Canada have experienced great difficulty integrating into progressive, equity-based coalitions due to racist, class, gendered, and other forms of discrimination embedded in these coalitions. Immigrants' ethnically based arguments for the preservation of language, culture, and family are a form of resistance to the limited and often absent routes to the achievement of better living and working conditions. Although it may be important to maintain some cultural traditions, promoting respect for these traditions is linked to a state multiculturalist discourse about the importance of respecting diversity. But the promotion of diversity does not in and of itself translate into better access to education, health, and jobs.

In order to further explore the relationship between nationalism and economic globalization, this chapter does several things. First, I explore the complex and sometimes contradictory discourse of Portuguese delegates to three conferences spanning two decades, in which they articulate their needs and concerns as citizens and immigrants. There is a distinct evolution from a focus on class, gender, and work in a 1982 conference, to a stronger celebration of Portuguese ethnic identity and a more limited recognition of the social, economic, and racist underpinnings of Canadian nationalism in the 1990s conferences. Second, I investigate the specific issue of the lack of access to education as a way of unravelling the economic and social relations of multiculturalism. Education and skills training are frequently described as essential in the current period of economic restructuring, when the workforce is expected to be flexible and to adapt rapidly to changing market conditions. Canadian government policy and recent changes to immigration policy express an orientation towards encouraging skilled immigrant workers. Yet it has been argued that the main factor determining access to the Canadian job market is not skill, so much as gender, class, national origin, race, ethnicity, and knowledge of official languages (Mojab: 1999: 126). The concept of skill itself has been challenged as not being intrinsic to a job, but rather 'constructed and negotiated through ideological and political processes,' which are then reproduced in the immigration process and used 'as the basis for designating people to different classes of unequal citizenship' (Arat-Koc 1999:211). Immigrant women in particular have been disadvantaged by the points system that devalues many of the gender-based skills they have acquired in their paid and unpaid work (Fincher et al. 1994; Januário 1988). Immigrants such as the Portuguese, who have been in Canada for many years, frequently have raised the issue of their critical lack of access not only to employment, but to various forms of education, from language and skills training for adult Portuguese immigrants, to high school, college, and university education for their children.

I begin with an analysis of the divergent appraisals of Portuguese ethnicity by participants in several conferences. This is followed by and juxtaposed to an assessment of the access to education of Portuguese first- and second-generation women and Canadian-born women. The interaction of these two phenomena indicates a framework for exploring the limitations of multiculturalist politics.

The Politics of Multiculturalism: Portuguese Perspectives

In this chapter I focus on three conferences:

• The 1982 conference, 'The Portuguese Community of Toronto:

Needs and Services,' sponsored by the Portuguese Interagency Network (PIN);

• The 1993 conference, 'From Coast to Coast: A Community in Transition,' organized by a broad range of Portuguese associations from across Canada;

• The 1997 conference, 'It's Time to Inherit the Future: Portuguese Canadian National Youth Conference,' organized by the Portuguese Canadian National Congress.

There is a clear difference between the conference that occurred in 1982 that focused on Toronto, and the two other conferences in the 1990s that had a national focus. The more local character of the earlier conference and its close association with the Portuguese Interagency Network – a community association allied with service providers based in Toronto – may have provided the impetus that gave it a political and activist agenda. Perhaps as important was the fact that the early 1980s were marked by labour unrest and strikes in the garment and cleaning industries in Toronto where many Portuguese immigrants worked. The keynote speaker at the conference defined the Portuguese in Toronto as being divided into two class groupings: 'The one to which the majority of the people belong is made of tens of thousands of members of the working class ... The other to which the minority belongs is made up of people who, because of the status they hold in the social, economic, educational and religious structure, fill positions of leadership and representation in the community' (PIN 1982:8). He argued that the Portuguese working class has not been divided because 'they were never agents of community identification as such' (ibid.). In other words, the working class identity of Portuguese immigrants was more important to them than their Portuguese ethnic identity, and, by extension, their subdivision into Azoreans and mainlanders. He questioned attempts to unify the Portuguese community as arising out of 'individualistic and selfish' concerns (ibid.): 'The question of unity or lack of unity is not a vital and conscious problem of the majority group' (ibid.:9).

The five workshops at the conference focused on inequities in education, health, and labour, and addressed the need for family/social and legal services. The workshop on labour issues raised the problem of integrating Portuguese workers not only into union membership, but also into leadership positions in the labour movement. Gender inequities confronted by Portuguese women in the labour force were also addressed, in particular, 'the lack of opportunities for skills training created by restrictive government legislation, and for entry into non-traditional occupations' (ibid.:29). The need for 'successor rights' in the cleaning and construction industries was highlighted. The existence of these rights ensures that when a new cleaning company takes over an existing cleaning contract for a building, the workers who had previously been employed become employees of the new cleaning company with the same conditions of work and pay. There have been ongoing attempts by employers to erode these rights. As one conference participant said: 'Their absence [of successor rights] may be viewed as a form of direct discrimination against Portuguese who constitute the majority of workers in the cleaning industry' (ibid.:29).

The difference in the politics of the 1982 and 1993 conferences is significant. The 1993 conference, 'From Coast to Coast: A Community in Transition,' aimed to establish a Portuguese Canadian National Congress in Canada, something that had been attempted in the late 1960s and abandoned by the early 1970s. Participants expressed a variety of perspectives within a multicultural state discourse that argued for the defence of 'Portuguese-Canadian interests' and advocated radical visions of citizenship and democracy. Some argued that the creation of a national organization would help to develop linkages between Portuguese across Canada, to preserve the Portuguese language and culture, and provide a strong lobby group to defend Portuguese-Canadian interests (Costa 1995:2). The conference report reveals significant interest in access to employment and education for Portuguese, and assertions by participants that Portuguese have received inequitable treatment in access to jobs, training, education, and other services (ibid.). However, there was little mention of the role of international economic restructuring or gender and class differences among Portuguese, unlike the earlier conference which devoted a good deal of attention to gender relations and participation in the labour movement (PIN 1982).

A keynote speaker at the 1993 conference, focused on the importance of 'integration' into Canada as a means of remedying inequities: 'We should then embrace the culture of our new home, integrating the day-to-day life of our hosts and taking advantage of the pleasurable environment of our new country' (Costa 1995:38).[2]

Although still advocating 'integration,' another participant was more cautious and critical. She argued for inclusion into a more utopian, Marshallian version of citizenship, combined with a radical view of democracy: '[I]ntegration is only achieved when all the members of a cultural community feel that they are real citizens, that is, that they have the same privileges, the same rights, access to the same resources and access to power, equal to that of those in power' (ibid.:45). At the same time, however, she expressed a sense of urgency that Portuguese speak 'with a single voice' in order to compete with immigrant groups arriving in Canada: 'Because we have been in the country for a long time and because immigration rates are low, our community is considered as not facing problems of integration. Priority and funding are thus provided to a new wave of immigrants formed by Turks, Russians, Sri Lankans, Asians, etc.' (ibid.:46).

Another participant felt it was extremely important to become part of the formal political process and to struggle for benefits for the Portuguese community *and* 'other ethnic groups' from within, while not bending to partisan politics. He was critical of ethnic nationalism, advocating a more progressive form of multiculturalism: 'Multiculturalism does not mean forming separate ghettoes or political blocs to fight each other – rather in my view, it's supposed to respect our differences, even encourage us to maintain our various identities, but also to work together to form a common national identity and strengthen our common political system' (ibid.:48).

However, the influence of state multiculturalism as a blueprint for the development of a Portuguese national association is evident in the desire to create an association that would emulate the structure of the Canadian Ethnocultural Council. This kind of structure would better enable the Portuguese in Canada to accomplish 'the dissemination of the Portuguese culture, in its multiple facets and the creation of new cultural forms relevant to our experiences' (ibid.:59).

The 1997 conference, 'It's Time to Inherit the Future,' was unique in its focus on Portuguese youth in Canada.[3] Many of the same concerns were raised in this conference as in the previous two, i.e., health, education, family, and employment. As with the 1992 conference, there was no mention of class difference, although racism and gender issues were discussed. At the 1997 conference issues of sexuality and HIV/AIDS were addressed for the first time. Organizers expressed a multiculturalist concern for 'motivating youth to take an active interest in their roots and future,' which was described as a particularly important goal for the 'older generation' who 'had witnessed their descendants lose interest and move away from traditional Portuguese culture' (Rolo 1998:1, 3).[4] The conference report indicates that one impetus for the conference came from the older generation who 'expressed disappointment in the proportional under-representation of Portuguese descendants in politics and professions regarded as prestigious and powerful' (Rolo 1998:3).

The older generation's association of culture/tradition with success was not critiqued or examined in the conference report, but remains as a reminder of the tension between generations on issues of culture, work, and achievement. Another concern of those who participated was the low attendance by youth. Two explanations were given in the conference report: '[L]imited enrolment was due to this being the first event of its kind for the generations targeted by 'It's Time to Inherit the Future' ... [or] ... as reflective of the lack of interest on the part of youth in anything Portuguese' (Rolo 1998:11).

It might be as important to know who did not attend, as it is to know who did. Most of the 'active and vocal' youth participants were university students (ibid.:8). There was little comment on the class implications of the limited participation of other young Portuguese women and men, except that 'the level of education and integration [of those who attended] is higher than that of the average community member' (Rolo 1998:10). I would argue that, in addition to the intimidation felt by working-class youth in taking part in such an event, Portuguese youth did not attend because their identities, for strategic reasons, are not strongly associated with the Portuguese community. That is, they may have decided that access to employment and education and other resources would not be facilitated by promoting their ethnic identity.[5] This brings us back to the questions raised in the 1982 conference regarding who represents and defines a group such as the Portuguese, which may be just as important as defining what it is to be Portuguese.

In *Thinking Through*, Himani Bannerji explores the *politics* of identity politics. She asks, 'Why do we want to be authentic so badly? What makes us think that an existence at any given moment is anything but authentic?' (1995:184). In responding to her own question, she writes: 'Our discomfort is with why we came at all, and why in this way – the 'why' referring to colonization, pulled along by the long chains of imperialism. It is not 'a free choice,' even when we are not refugees. This is a dance of power, if not always a dance of death. We enter preorganized terrains, the same terms hold here as in trade and financial relations between Western capitalism and the Third World' (ibid.).

Assuming the terms of the relationship between immigrants and the Canadian state are reflected in international restructuring relationships, then forms of resistance need to move beyond struggles for cultural authenticity to broader-based solidarities that accept difference, but are able to recognize and resist the effects of international restructuring locally, nationally, and internationally. This conclusion is similar to the arguments made by participants to the 1982 conference. But this goal is not easily accomplished. Activists and those who become community leaders/workers in immigrant organizations funded by the state must assume the cloak of state multicultural discourse in order to access the resources needed by immigrants and their families. In the 1990s, a 'mainstreaming' of multiculturalism was accompanied by the de-funding of ethno-specific community groups and led to the further incorporation of these groups into mainstream organizations with state-defined multicultural agendas (Das Gupta 1999:203). The roles of community activist organizations were now defined in a dualistic way in partnership with mainstream organizations. Although the personal histories of many community activists as immigrant workers, or de-scendants of immigrant workers and feminists, may lead many to be critical of an imposed, state-defined multicultural discourse, they now have been cornered into arguing on an ethnic (rather than a class, gender, and racialized) basis, i.e., as Portuguese-Canadians. Defunded 'partners' have less clout in arguing for better access to schools and university education, skills, and language training.

Like the Chinese in Vancouver, who in some historical periods – in particular during the recent years of multiculturalism in Canada – have strategically 'consented to and even appropriated' the identity and stereotypes that defined their subordination (Anderson 1991:27),[6] Portuguese have accessed scarce state resources by using their 'Portu-gueseness.' For example, at the 1993 conference some argued for a national organization under the umbrella of Canada's multicultural policy. At other times, Portuguese have fiercely resisted racist stereo-types, such as 'the hardworking Portuguese,' which, as a participant at the 1993 conference pointed out, were not reflected in promotions or job upgrading (Costa 1995:24). When possible, some Portuguese have joined labour movements to resist unfair labour practices and have struggled against racism and class discrimination in the Canadian education system that historically has streamed their children. But the labour movement, feminist, anti-racist, education, and health coalitions have not always been accessible or attractive alternatives for Portuguese immigrants and their descendants. As many of the case studies in this book have demonstrated, the barriers to participation in these move-ments and coalitions are not solely the responsibility of the immigrant family, but also rest with the state, the labour movement, and the non-governmental sector (e.g., a lack of access to language training; ethnic, racist, and gender discrimination in unions; a lack of understanding/ concern for the specific physical/emotional health, safety, and educational needs of immigrant workers, their families, and, especially, youth). A critique of Canadian multiculturalism cannot be separated from the relationship of Portuguese to these other ways of identification that revolve around class, gender, and anti-racist struggles.

The Politics of Education

Intrinsic to multiculturalism and one of its instruments, immigration policy, is the creation of discrete ethnic groups that can be controlled and a masking of the reality that immigrant workers and their families are indeed part of the nation-state into which they have immigrated. Education is a means of instructing a group in a specific form of nationalism, and excluding groups of people from resources available to dominant or elite groups. That labour migration is a strategy to acquire cheap workers is made obvious by the fact that many countries have done little to upgrade the education and skills of immigrants. Research by Baganha reveals that, of those Portuguese men and women emigrants who return to Portugal from living and working abroad, 12 per cent are illiterate, 24 per cent have no formal schooling, and 56 per cent have acquired only primary schooling (1998:200). In stark contrast to the aforementioned figures, statistics for Canadian-born today indicate that, among the population aged 25 to 44 years old, 79 per cent have completed high school (Statistics Canada, *The Daily*. April 14, 1998).[7]

Factors both internal and external to the Portuguese household have prevented many women from gaining further education and what they consider to be better jobs. Internally, household and family gender relations, attitudes towards education, insufficient economic resources, class, age, and the number of dependants create barriers to education. Externally, inadequate language and employment training resources, unequal access to education due to immigration status and racialization, and gendered attitudes vis-à-vis education in the country of origin, all contribute towards difficulties in accessing education. Canadian employers have expressed traditional views of where women belong in the labour force, and thus employment equity issues have intersected with access to education and specialized skills training for women.

Education has been one of the issues most often identified by the

Portuguese as crucial to their future well-being (Nunes 1998, 1999). In the following pages, I begin with an analysis of Statistics Canada data, comparing the educational achievement of Portuguese-born women and men with foreign-born and Canadian-born between 1981 and 1996 (see Table 5.1). Following this, I use my own interview findings to explore access to education from the perspectives of first- and second-generation Portuguese women and compare their views and experiences with those of a group of Canadian-born, anglophone working-class women in Toronto.

In 1981 almost 60 per cent of Portuguese foreign-born women in Canada[8] had achieved no more than elementary school (up to 8 years of school) (see Table 5.1). By 1996, this figure had begun to improve, down to 47 per cent, as more recent entrants to this group gained access to secondary and post-secondary education either in Portugal or in Canada. In comparison to other foreign-born women, Portuguese foreign-born women lag far behind in educational attainment, except at the secondary level, where approximately equal percentages of women from both groups are located (e.g., in 1996, secondary school was the highest level of educational attainment for 35 per cent of Portuguese foreign-born women and 36 per cent of all other foreign-born women). The statistics in Table 5.1 demonstrate that from 1981 to 1996, Portuguese foreign-born immigrants made slight gains in access to higher levels of education, with women faring marginally better than men at the highest levels.

Portuguese Canadian-born have been able to make the greatest gains over the period (1986–91) in attaining college or university diplomas: an increase of 23 per cent in the proportion of women, and an increase of 21 per cent in the proportion of men over this time. During the same period, more Portuguese Canadian-born women than men were able to attain college or university levels of education. This gender gap is increasing in favour of the women: by 1996 it had reached 11 per cent. By comparison, at the college and university levels, the gender gap is disappearing for the general population. Similar percentages of the Portuguese Canadian-born and all other Canadian-born female populations are now achieving college or university levels of education. In fact, the Portuguese Canadian-born women were slightly ahead, at 49 per cent compared to 47 per cent for all other Canadian-born women, in 1996. However, there is a significant distance between the percentage of Portuguese Canadian-born men (38%) who have attained college or university levels of education and all other Canadian-born men (46%). My qualitative data explores the reasons behind these differences and similarities in educational attainments.

TABLE 5.1

Highest Level of Education by Gender and Ethnic Origin[a] / Place of Birth for Population 15 Years and Older (percentage of ethnic origin / place of birth), 1981–96

Highest Level of Education	Gender	Ethnic Origin / Place of Birth	1981 %	1986 %	1991 %	1996 %
Elementary (up to grade 8)	Female	Portuguese Foreign-Born	58.20	53.90	49.40	46.50
		Portuguese Canadian-Born	6.40	2.30	3.10	3.10
		All Other Foreign-Born	27.70	24.70	18.80	16.40
		All Other Canadian-Born	18.50	15.60	12.10	10.40
		Total	20.50	17.50	14.20	12.40
	Male	Portuguese Foreign-Born	51.80	45.10	44.40	42.20
		Portuguese Canadian-Born	9.20	6.20	3.10	2.40
		All Other Foreign-Born	21.70	18.90	16.40	13.90
		All Other Canadian-Born	18.70	16.00	12.20	10.50
		Total	19.50	16.70	13.60	11.60
Secondary (including high school diploma and trades certificate at secondary level)	Female	Portuguese Foreign-Born	30.30	32.40	34.10	34.80
		Portuguese Canadian-Born	68.10	75.30	62.10	48.30
		All Other Foreign-Born	37.10	36.40	38.70	36.30
		All Other Canadian-Born	47.60	46.20	45.30	42.40
		Total	45.50	44.30	43.40	40.60
	Male	Portuguese Foreign-Born	31.80	37.50	36.60	38.30
		Portuguese Canadian-Born	73.60	68.90	67.50	59.60
		All Other Foreign-Born	32.60	31.80	36.00	34.70
		All Other Canadian-Born	45.50	44.10	45.10	43.50
		Total	43.00	41.80	42.50	41.00

TABLE 5.1 *(Concluded)*
Highest Level of Education by Gender and Ethnic Origin[a]/Place of Birth for Population 15 Years and Older
(percentage of ethnic origin/place of birth), 1981–96

Highest Level of Education	Gender	Ethnic Origin / Place of Birth	1981 %	1986 %	1991 %	1996 %
College or University	Female	Portuguese Foreign-Born	11.50	13.70	16.50	18.70
		Portuguese Canadian-Born	25.50	22.40	34.80	48.60
		All Other Foreign-Born	35.20	39.00	42.50	47.30
		All Other Canadian-Born	33.90	38.20	42.60	47.20
		Total	34.00	38.20	42.40	47.00
	Male	Portuguese Foreign-Born	16.50	17.50	19.00	19.50
		Portuguese Canadian-Born	17.20	24.80	29.40	37.90
		All Other Foreign-Born	45.70	49.30	47.60	51.40
		All Other Canadian-Born	35.80	39.90	42.70	46.10
		Total	37.50	41.50	43.90	47.40

Notes:

a. Only those reporting Portuguese-only are included in the Portuguese ethnic group.

Source: Based on a 2–3% sample of the Canadian population in Statistics Canada, Public Use Sample Tapes (1981) and Public Use Microdata Files (1986, 1991, 1996)

First- and second-generation Portuguese women interviewed in Toronto have divergent views regarding education and their access to it. Both groups of women evaluate education at least partly in terms of how it conflicts or harmonizes with values that are important to the family and that are regarded as essential to the survival of the household. For a first-generation woman, whose role as a mother and a wife is described as paramount, attending school might be an attractive idea, but taking care of the household through unpaid domestic labour and paid jobs often is deemed more important. Efforts to keep the family united, with the common goal of increasing material welfare as quickly as possible, sometimes has blocked Portuguese women of both generations from upgrading their education. The extent to which immigration policy consigns this housewife role to Portuguese women is an important issue. Canadian immigration policy traditionally has defined most women as dependents of men (or as sponsored immigrants) and as 'not destined for the labour force.' This identity impedes their access to those language and skills training opportunities related to entry to the paid workforce. Only certain types of paid work are defined as skilled and worth rewarding with preferred types of language training and skills upgrading. Labour market language training programs (as opposed to training in basic communication skills) provide specialized or advanced language training oriented to labour market needs and directed to those who have labour market skills 'in demand.' Portuguese women, who have been mainly dependent immigrants, have been less able to access these courses than independent immigrants, who are mostly men.

Second-generation women have been more able to gain access to education than their parents. In some cases they are unsuccessful in gaining their parents' support for their own educational aspirations. Sometimes their spouses oppose their further education. Casting back to the 1930s in the U.S., Bodnar describes how eastern and southern European working-class immigrants 'sacrificed individual inclinations to family needs' (1980:48) in similar ways to Portuguese first-generation immigrants who have eschewed the possibilities of further educating themselves in Canada. Bodnar calls this 'working-class realism' (ibid.), or pragmatism in the face of limited opportunities. He claims that, for these groups of immigrants, skilled backgrounds were less important than networks in acquiring employment (ibid.:51). However, there is also ample evidence in the case studies in this book and elsewhere that many Portuguese first-generation parents in Canada are anxious that their children succeed academically (Nunes 1998:27, 1999;

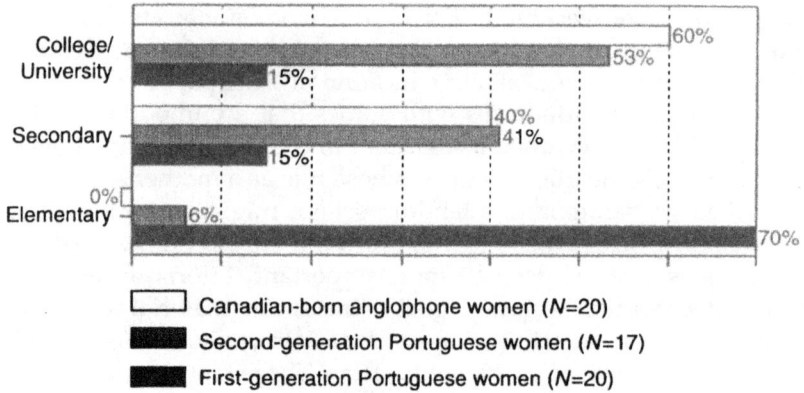

*By percentage of women in each level of education

Note: At the time they were interviewed in Toronto, the Canadian-born women ranged in age from 27 to 56; the second-generation women ranged in age from 22 to 39; the first-generation women were between 32 and 59 .

Figure 5.1. Highest Level of Education: Comparison among Three Groups of Women Interviewed*

Noivo 1997:88–90; Agiuar 1994), and that they wanted more education for themselves.

In a parallel study, carried out on Canadian-born, anglophone working-class women, these women were found to be less emotionally and economically tied to their parents' home than were second-generation Portuguese women. Their families often were composed of their immediate children and their friends. Their prioritization of education was based on long-term planning for their personal future. Their approach was more individualized than that of Portuguese women. The Canadian-born women did not express concern about the attitudes of family or friends regarding access to education, but referred instead to other struggles outside of their households. They made greater use of social services – housing, bridging programs (to college and university), and help for single-support mothers – than did Portuguese women. These women achieved slightly more years of education than did second-generation Portuguese women.

First-Generation Portuguese women

As described in Chapter One, most first-generation women had little

access to education in Portugal before arriving in Canada. My interview data indicate an average of 3–7 years. Figure 5.1 demonstrates that
most of the women interviewed (70%) had less than nine years of
education; in fact, most had less than five years of education. The rest
(15%) were divided evenly between those completing high school,
college, or university. These figures are comparable to figures for Third
World countries such as Algeria and Zambia where respectively, 80 per
cent and 74 per cent of women aged 25 years and older are illiterate
(Seager 1997:85, UN Statistics Division 2000:gender/4-1afr.htm). In
contrast, in 1995, Canada ranked highest internationally in school life
expectancy, at 16.5 years for men and 17.1 years for women (United
Nations Statistics Division 2000:social/education.htm). Canada also in-
vests more in education than do most other industrialized nations (Galt
2000:A10). Yet, disturbingly, Portuguese immigrant women fare as poorly
in Canada as they would in Zambia, where the school life expectancy
for women is 7.2 years (United Nations Statistics Division 2000:ibid.).

Figure 5.1 indicates that the turning point for further education for
Portuguese first-generation women was the end of elementary school,
not high school, as it was for the two other groups. This is an indication
that for most families in rural Portugal, as soon as children were strong
enough to do manual labour, work on the family farm or business in
Portugal took precedence over education. In addition, many families
simply could not afford the fees that were charged in post-elementary
school. Most of those interviewed who did manage to move past elementary school went through high school; some went to college or
university. However, this should not be taken as a reflection of the way
Portuguese first-generation women evaluate educational achievement
in the urban industrial setting of Toronto. Augusta, a union organizer,
in retrospect, expresses her naivety about working and living in Canada,
and her regret about her lack of formal schooling:

> For those few years before I left Portugal I didn't even bother going to
> higher school over there. Because oh, you're going to Canada – what's the
> use? You don't need it. Right now I think I need it. Whatever you get in
> one country counts in another. So I only got to grade 4. People felt that
> because Canada was English and Portugal was Portuguese you just didn't
> need any more education in Portugal.

Lacking a sufficient understanding of the benefits of education,
Augusta arrived in Canada already at a disadvantage. In Canada,
like many other first-generation Portuguese immigrants, she did not

return to school and was unable to take advantage of English language classes:

> It's very depressing at the beginning because you don't speak English. You kind of get used to it then and you start to learn a few words and then you make friends ... and you sort of live a Portuguese life in a Canadian country – in Toronto, right? So it's more or less like you don't need the English.

For first-generation women like Augusta, ensuring the future success of her younger siblings has meant giving up thoughts of further education for herself. This choice was not without disappointment:

> I kind of decided not to go to school because I wanted to earn money and help my three other sisters and brothers go to school. Now I regret it and maybe I should have done it.

For some women such as Fatima, a nurse's aid, the workplace language training which she was able to take was very important. In the end, she was able to convince her sceptical husband of the value of further education:

> I used to go to school to learn English and the course was paid by the hospital, twice a week, two hours a day, and they'd also pay me the time during work hours – I did this at George Brown – and my husband wasn't very happy. I don't know, he's not a person who has a lot of ambition in life. What I do is enough for him, but not for me. After I went to school, he came to understand me. I didn't have a big problem because of that, but in the beginning he used to say that I didn't need to learn more than what I had.

Fatima's aspirations extended far beyond language training classes to becoming a professional nurse. But she had a dilemma – whether to support her children through university or educate herself. She was doubtful about how to achieve both, and in the end opted for supporting her children, giving her age as a reason:

> I'm satisfied with this work but I'd like to return to school, I'd like to become a nurse, but I only felt this vocation after I started working at the hospital. But not right now and as a matter of fact I may not even ever go back to school, because my son is about to go to university and he needs

my help, and then when he's finished, my daughter will start. By the time she's finished, who knows? Perhaps I'm already too old for that right now.

Many other women have not been successful in convincing their spouses of the value of education. Januaria, a cleaner, describes how her husband controlled her and limited her personal development by confirming her domestic responsibilities. Women's isolation in their households diminishes the possibility of resistance to this control:

I never went to English school in Canada – my husband didn't want me to go out at night. It's not because of the children, because they are old enough now and they can be home by themselves. He wanted to go to night school too, and I said, 'No, you can't. You don't have the right. If I can't go, then you can't go either.' I told him, 'Why can't I go with the lady who is your cousin's wife?' He said, 'No.' She used to come by to pick me up, but I told her, 'No, he doesn't want me to go.' And nowadays she can speak English and she can write it too. And I don't know anything.

Second-Generation Portuguese Women

Second-generation Portuguese women all have gone to school in Canada; most of those interviewed had finished high school and attended some college and university courses (see Figure 5.1). In comparison to the non-immigrant working-class women interviewed in the early 1990s, slightly fewer second-generation Portuguese women had achieved a college or university education (53%) than the former (60%). One Portuguese woman had a university degree, eight had completed a college diploma, and four left college or university before receiving a degree. It is notable, in Statistics Canada data, that the proportion of Canadian-born Portuguese women who achieved a university or college education increased by 14 per cent from 1991–6 (see Table 5.1).

The women interviewed in the early 1990s had mixed experiences regarding the attitudes of their parents towards education. Some described their parents as discouraging them from attending college or university, or even from finishing high school. However, several of the women talked about the importance their parents attached to education, but these parents were described as 'non-traditional' by Eunice, who is now a bank worker:

If they came from very traditional families where emphasis was placed on marriage and family, then they would not really care about academic achievement, and many would just go to a high school like Central Commerce where you learn a specific trade or skill and after that – grade 12 – you go into the workplace. Whereas a couple of my other Portuguese friends came from a more non-traditional family, where parents emphasized academic achievement. Their mentality was such that they would work towards that goal, going to the best elementary school, the best high school, the best university, and perhaps an attempt at a non-traditional role.

Rosa, a social worker, describes being discouraged by her parents from attending university:

I didn't want to go to university. I didn't want to do anything complicated because I didn't think I could handle it. We weren't encouraged to feel like we could succeed at anything. We weren't made to feel that we could go to university and do really well and that was what our goal should be. [O]ur training as children in the family was that you got to get a job that's going to keep you alive to survive and that's what is important in life.

She raises the importance of parents' class as a factor in whether they encouraged their children to seek higher education:

Someone like Maria may have been raised in a higher class than I was and that's why she's been able to have access to the university.

However, in spite of her parents' disapproval, Rosa finished high school at night school and attended college, where she studied social work.

Rosie, a receptionist, also returned to finish high school later in her life. She said that her husband and his family, as well as her parents, opposed her further education:

I had to fight to go to school. My husband did not support that. It took me seven years to do my psychology. I started that in '81 and finished in '88. I did my psychology between 10:00 p.m. and 1:00 in the morning, after I did a full day's work ... got home ... did everything ... got the baby to bed and that's when I sat down and did all my assignments. I got a certificate in psychology. My dream was to go back to a university. My husband said I was crazy and the extended family were very negative – they said I was crazy. The first generation – our parents – are very negative about school. Even today his parents, they started laughing. They didn't believe it.

Some Portuguese second-generation women who have not finished high school, such as Rosalia, who works as a babysitter, expressed a sense of both loss and resignation at not returning to finish school:

> What I really regret now is that I didn't stay in school longer, because I never went to high school, so nowadays I'm sorry. It's not too late now, but I don't care now anymore. Some time ago I would have liked to have been something else, professionally.

The trajectory for these second-generation women is different from their mothers. Overall, they tend to be much better educated, and the majority value education, even though they may have been unable to access it to their satisfaction. Although some, such as Ricarda, a legal secretary, are disappointed that they were unable to achieve more, they feel certain that their children will be well educated:

> We're the sandwich generation. There's resentment for the first generation and probably resentment for the third, because they're getting what we should have got ... our children are getting the benefits of what we didn't reap and sow. They're getting the university education.

But a university education cannot prevent gender discrimination by Canadian employers. Although most Portuguese second-generation women trained for traditional female sectors of the labour force, some who trained in non-traditional sectors, nevertheless found themselves placed in traditional female sectors. For example, Felicidade trained in electronics, but worked as a receptionist:

> After my computer-electronics course – I was lucky – the first interview I went to, I got the job. It helped that I had electronics. I started installing their phones. I also used to help out at the office and the manager said to me, 'You're good. Let's bring you up here.' So now I'm in the office. I'm not using my electronic skills at all.

Emilia, who trained as a computer programmer, was influenced both by a job offer and by her mother's encouragement and now works as an office coordinator:

> This is my first full-time job. I had finished my computer programming job and I was thinking of applying to different companies to become a compu-

ter programmer and then I thought, 'Well, I don't have enough experience.' And then someone from St Mary's [community centre] approached me to be an office coordinator. I thought if I worked at St Mary's I might not have the opportunity to become a computer programmer. And then my mom said, 'Well, I think it's a better idea because you haven't worked before.'

Canadian-Born Women

The Canadian-born anglophone women I interviewed all described themselves as working-class women. Their average earnings were $27,000 and ranged from $14,000 to $40,000. In general, they had engaged in many unskilled or semi-skilled jobs in a variety of work sectors, depending upon where they were living and their personal contacts. At the time they were interviewed these women had worked in clerical, retail, domestic cleaning, and childcare, as well as union organizing and teaching ESL. Most had left school early, some as early as 15 years of age. A minority had gone on immediately to finish high school and then college or university. The pattern for many of these women included a return to education as adults, either through their workplace or on their own, often as single parents with a minimum of financial resources. In fact, at the time I interviewed these women, 60 per cent had achieved a university or college degree (see Figure 5.1).[9]

Susan, a thirty-year-old receptionist, described an abusive family life, dropping out of school before she graduated, working at seven or eight consecutive jobs, including waitressing, working in sales and administration at Eaton's, and then making several unsuccessful attempts at re-entering school. She has finally been successful at finishing high school and is confidently looking forward to university:

> I have applied for Engineering, Science, and Business, and I have also applied for Management Economics at Waterloo. I'm expected to get accepted in at least two of those ... I don't know which I'm going to pick yet. But what I would like to do down the road, after getting my education, sometime, ten years later, is to start my own consulting business.

Caroline, a twenty-seven-year-old cleaner, also from an abusive family, dropped out of school and was living on the street by the time she was 14 years old. She had her first child when she was 17 and two others after. She gave up one child for adoption. She is a single parent, now in her third year of high school, and is interested in pursuing studies in university:

Generally I'm a 90 per cent student, like an 'A' student. Once in a while I'm in the 80's. I work until the last minute to draw something together. It will take me a few years until I toughen up my [study] habits ... I want to work in Sociology. Psychiatry is okay, but I like groups of people and, as much as I'm interested in individual people, I'm also interested in things like the penal system, jails, or mental institutions. I have a lot of friends who are schizophrenic, manic-depressive; they have compulsive disorders.

Over the years she has had access to a variety of social services, ranging from housing assistance to programs for sole support mothers. At present she cleans part time and has lived in the same co-op housing with her children for about eight years.

Carol, a women in her forties who works as an inspector in the Public Works Department, left school before finishing grade 12. She first became a clerical worker and then retrained for her present job. As she said:

The way that I got this position was that I took a training program at the city called Bridges for non-traditional work. I was in the first class. There were thirty-four days of training which includes a week at George Brown and a three-week work placement, where I selected building inspection. But it is a highly skilled job. So I started at Ryerson and I took construction in the fall. I signed up for Drafting. It is a higher skilled job, a higher paid job. For me to switch from one profession [clerical work] to another is like a career path. I changed as a person.

Their ability to access education and better jobs has changed over the course of adulthood for these women, particularly if they have been able to use state services in the areas of childcare, retraining, and personal counselling. Traditional family ties are not always as important to them as friendship or community relationships, and there is less emphasis on their economic and social contribution to the 'family' unit than there is in the lives of Portuguese women. Both Portuguese second-generation women and the Canadian-born anglophone women described a home life that often was fractured by intergenerational dissent and abuse. Yet the Portuguese were more likely to remain at their parents' home, or to return home after a temporary absence, whereas the Canadian-born women left permanently to set up their own households, separate from their parents.

The ways in which the three groups of women described themselves, their experiences, and their need for education have implications for the effects of restructuring on their lives. In this regard, the process of naming oneself as Portuguese, working-class, and/or Canadian is significant. Rosalind Brunt (1989, in Yuval-Davis 1994:415) asks how our identities are represented in and through the culture and are assigned particular categories, as well as who or what represents us politically. These representations may be introduced as homogeneous or unitary, and thus essentialist, particularly if they form part of a public multicultural discourse. However, they may be part of a nascent politics whereby naming oneself as part of a collective is a political act and will affect access to strategic state resources, such as childcare and mother's allowance, which are often essential to the accessing of education.

These resources are more available to some groups of women than to others, depending upon ethnicity, race, and class. Mojab (1999:123) argues that deskilling and skilling coexist in the drive for the maximization of profit, so that immigrants with financial resources and from certain regions (e.g., the U.S., Australia, or Britain) are able to access skills upgrading, while others are not. Richmond's research on Caribbean immigrants to Canada (1990) indicates that racism in the Ontario school system has been an obstacle to the academic achievement of Caribbean students, particularly those born outside of Canada, whose underachievement exists regardless of the socio-economic status of their parents. Portuguese immigrants are also among those who, for racist reasons, have been unable to access adult education for themselves. Their situation likens Canada to a Third World country.

Conclusion

There is a close association between access to education and the politics of state multiculturalism. Although respect for cultural difference is important, the promotion of a particular ethnic identity, such as a Portuguese identity, has not and will not lead to more equitable access to basic resources such as education unless it is linked to more broadly based struggles against racism, and gender and class inequities.

As demonstrated by the three conferences described earlier, Portuguese in recent years, seem to be making stronger multiculturalist arguments for recognition of their unique ethnic identity, while arguing against the racialization of Portuguese in Canada. As the discourse of the participants in these conferences indicates, Portuguese in Canada, like other immigrant groups, are divided on the direction their struggles should take: whether towards a promotion of cultural authenticity or towards broader-based solidarities. There may be a third way of identifying, which combines various communities of resistance, including the cultural, but with different goals and priorities than those envisaged by a state multiculturalist framework. It is possible to move beyond isolated struggles based on ethnicity or ethnic identity to multifaceted local, national, and international movements that can address more vigorously social inequities in education, employment, and health through collective forms of resistance.

The next chapter concludes the book by taking a closer look at the relationship between nationalism, multiculturalism, and exclusionary practices. It also explores some of the possibilities for resistance and for change towards more equitable living and working conditions.

Chapter Six

Conclusion – Nationalisms and Differences

In this final chapter I attempt to bring together the three themes that have shaped my argument. First, the life histories, case studies, and statistical data, particularly as defined in Chapters One through Four, constitute a critique of essentialist frameworks that define Portuguese and other immigrants and their descendants in unitary, homogeneous ways that become the basis for an unequal distribution of state resources. Canadian immigration and multicultural state policy have demonstrated little enthusiasm for recognizing and addressing the needs of Portuguese women as immigrant *workers* who are part of a restructuring industrial workforce. Second, the renegotiation of citizenship that is part and parcel of global migration will continue to be a crucial concern as labour persists as a primary trading commodity. Despite the claims by the Canadian government that only highly skilled, English/ French speaking immigrants will be welcomed to this country in the future, those who are defined otherwise will certainly continue to arrive at our borders and challenge our citizenship practices. The depiction of the working lives and struggles of Portuguese women immigrants in Chapter Four and their efforts to achieve equal opportunities in education in Chapter Five, challenge claims to the existence of liberal notions of citizenship in Canada. Third, the theme of nationalism that filters through the entire book is addressed directly in Chapter Five and in this chapter, in which I explore the limitations of both Portuguese and Canadian nationalisms. Multiculturalism in Canada is imbued with a nationalist discourse that is gendered and familialistic, while masking economic restructuring and its consequences for immigrants and their descendants. Portuguese nationalism, linking its emigrants back to Portugal through a web of cultural, economic, political, and social relationships which are characterized by regionalism and expressed in remittances and return migration is a kind of survival strategy and form of resistance by working-class immigrants to the alienation and oppressiveness of capitalism.

This concluding chapter begins by re-examining issues of remittances, return migration, and regionalism on the part of Portuguese immigrants to Canada, topics that recur in many of the case studies in this book. This is followed by an analysis of state multiculturalist practices from Canadian and global perspectives, and final comments on struggle and resistance.

Nationalist Politics of Remittances, Return, and Regionalism

Decisions to remit money or return to Portugal are characterized by a regionalism that divides Portugal into the more poorly developed Azorean islands and the wealthier mainland. Remittances and return migration to the home country are linked forms of limited resistance to capitalist economic boundaries and demonstrate the instability and complexity of this fractured expression of Portuguese nationalism and ultimately, its social, political, and economic underpinnings.

Seen through the lens of remittance obligations, Portugal has an ambiguous relationship with emigrants. On the one hand, the Portuguese state, through its nationalist discourse, must maintain a delicate balance between encouraging emigrants to remain elsewhere, in order to remit needed infusions of foreign capital and, on the other hand, ensuring émigrés' continued allegiance and ties to Portugal in order to secure the endurance of these remittances. Thus government discourse stresses the importance of sending remittances in order to prepare for a return home, but does little in an institutional way to support the reintegration of returnees (Rocha-Trindade 1993:273). As well, the gender relations of Portuguese nationalism, like other forms of nationalism, have less to offer women economically and politically than men.

Some first-generation women and/or their husbands travel to Portugal on holidays and build houses there. Now, however, they regard a return to Portugal, part of the European Community, as economically difficult for the immigrant who returns with Canadian dollars:

I have that objective: sell what we have and buy a house there or a flat. Now we go to Portugal every two years. We see big changes, for the best.

It's bad for the immigrant, because everything is more expensive. (Clarisse, first-generation, jewelery factory worker, mainland)

Although Portuguese first-generation immigrants in Toronto may regard Portugal as a place to which they will retire, their travel there may not be frequent. Some women had not returned at all to Portugal, and yet were building homes or planning to build homes and retire there. Differing attitudes towards returning to Portugal between women from the Azores and the Portuguese mainland are associated with several issues. The type of wage work available to women in the Azores is more limited than the more varied opportunities on the mainland; economic, educational, and social possibilities for women in the Azores are also more limited than on the mainland, which is more connected to the European Community than the Azores. Finally, some Portuguese women in Canada have achieved a certain economic and social independence that is more likely to be matched on the Portuguese mainland than in the Azores, where the history of politics and religion have been conservative, and women are more closely tied to their households than on the mainland. Unlike second-generation women, this generation engages with Portugal through a household insularity in Canada in which a Portuguese world view is nurtured and maintained by spouses, children, and other relatives located in close proximity, as well as by associations with an extended, and to a certain extent, 'imagined community' in Portugal.

Second-generation Portuguese do not express the same ties to the land of Portugal as do first-generation immigrants. However, although the allegiances of second-generation Portuguese are directed outward, in many cases away from the Portuguese community and household in Toronto, they still identify themselves as Portuguese. Their experiences involve a degree of rejection of some aspects of the culture and politics of the older generation and are interwoven with struggles to overcome the stereotyping they encounter in Canada as second-generation Portuguese. They neither accept wholly the culture of their parents nor a Canadian cultural identity.

One community worker noted that the differences in the economic and social contexts of the two regions from which the immigrants originated had an important effect on the attitudes of Portuguese towards their lives in Canada:

There is a gap between people from the mainland and people from the

Azores. The Azoreans feel, and rightly so, that they were neglected. And when they come here, they tend to be very content with what you give them. Most of the people from the mainland when I talk to them they say, 'Well, Canada is good but there are a lot of things that are not very good – especially the moral fibre.' They are all concerned about children and so forth. But people from the Azores very rarely do they say anything bad about Canada. (Cora Perreira, community worker/activist)

The ambiguity of nationalist sentiments as described above reflects a mixture of concerns about basic economic survival, morality, and raising children. But more importantly, it defines how Portuguese colonial attitudes towards the Azores islands differentiate that group from other Portuguese immigrants. Costa points out that Azorean Portuguese experience alienation vis-à-vis both Portugal and Canada:

I've seen Azorean families from outside of Toronto who have lost, completely, their identity with Portugal. I have been amazed at that. I've seen mainland families [from the Portuguese mainland] who live 15 years up in Timmins, for example, and those kids speak Portuguese perfectly and talk about Portugal perfectly. What I mean is that the mainlanders might even be proud of what they know about Portugal, even though they feel Canadian. And the Azoreans will not know anything about Portugal and the Azores, but also feel an alien. It's a mixture of a lot of things. (Jaime Costa, community worker)

Costa discusses in more detail the way in which children are defined as being at the centre of questions about the retention and transference of Portuguese nationalist identity and 'values,' particularly for those from mainland Portugal:

Many children who are born here [Toronto] to a Portuguese family, for two or three years they are really touched by the Portuguese culture only. And then for the next six years, when he or she is in primary school, all the values, all the fears of this Portuguese family are implanted into this child. [W]hen he or she becomes 16, 17, 18, and you ask them a question and they will say, yes I'm Canadian first, but I'm Portuguese. They see the duality. Especially if they're from the mainland. Because many parents are from the mainland, they still want to have these children prepared to go back to Portugal. And they want them even to have their studies organized in Portugal – the language and everything. I think this happens more with Portuguese families who live in Toronto than the ones who are away from Toronto [in smaller towns and rural areas]. (Jaime Costa, community worker/activist)[1]

Costa describes the transference of culture as incorporating a fear of the other, which is also a fear of losing certain aspects of one's culture. A desire to return to Portugal for those from the mainland is thus defined through this fear of loss of language and Portuguese values. The idea of returning becomes part of the processual character of migration for these immigrants.

The examples of remittances, return migration, and regionalism demonstrate the complexity and tenuousness of the idea of a unified Portuguese nationalism. Gender relations also contribute to the complex nature of this nationalism and to decisions about a return to Portugal, as do economic restructuring policies. Although economic restructuring and the education of children may cause some emigrants to return home to Portugal, other factors, as described above, lead them to stay in Canada, which may result in a cessation of remittances to Portugal. Thus, behind the facade of Portuguese nationalism are the economic and social relations and realities of migration that define its actual purpose, its success or failure.

In my analysis of difference within the Portuguese community, I have relied on Bottomley's use of Bourdieu's concept of 'habitus' and its manifestation in practice (what people do), as being 'polythetic' (many positioned). Using the example of Australia, Bottomley argues that 'in theory and to some extent in practice,' pluralistic forms of (non-state) multiculturalism have the potential of challenging nationalistically imagined communities. She states that despite the ardent efforts of 'defenders of Anglomorphism ... the social – and even the biological – reality of the Australian population is one of heterogeneity and hybridity. At last count, 67.3% of the population described their ethnic origins as mixed English and something else. Ethnic purity, therefore, is increasingly illusory and the same can be said of cultural purity' (1995a:15–16). Thus, in practice, there is 'recognition of the diversity of subjective positions and cultural identities' (Sarup 1994:103) that challenge norms stressing similarity, although nationalist discourses might indicate otherwise. Likewise, the percentage of Portuguese who identify themselves only as Portuguese compared to those who identify themselves in a mixed way as Portuguese and something else is changing in Canada (Table 6.1).

TABLE 6.1
Portuguese Population in Seven Major Census Metropolitan Areas (CMA), Single vs Multiple Response (count and as percentage within gender), 1986–96

CMA		1986 Single	1986 Multiple	1991 Single	1991 Multiple	1996 Single	1996 Multiple	% Change 1986–96 (Multiple Response)
Montreal	Female	266 88.96%	33 11.04%	461 86.98%	69 13.02%	429 80.94%	101 19.06%	8.02
	Male	260 91.55%	24 8.45%	467 88.78%	59 11.22%	461 80.59%	111 19.41%	10.95
	Total	526 90.22%	57 9.78%	928 87.88%	128 12.12%	890 80.76%	212 19.24%	9.46
Ottawa-Hull	Female	54 87.10%	8 12.90%	94 78.99%	25 21.01%	70 69.31%	31 30.69%	17.79
	Male	75 85.23%	13 14.77%	104 84.55%	19 15.45%	83 73.45%	30 26.55%	11.78
	Total	129 86.00%	21 14.00%	198 81.82%	44 18.18%	153 71.50%	61 28.50%	14.50
Toronto	Female	939 87.43%	135 12.57%	1858 87.23%	272 12.77%	1752 79.75%	445 20.25%	7.69
	Male	994 87.42%	143 12.58%	1874 88.35%	247 11.65%	1793 79.34%	467 20.66%	8.09
	Total	1933 87.43%	278 12.57%	3732 87.79%	519 12.21%	3545 79.54%	912 20.46%	7.89
Winnipeg	Female	58 85.29%	10 14.71%	112 88.19%	15 11.81%	97 82.91%	20 17.09%	2.39
	Male	80 87.91%	11 12.09%	124 88.57%	16 11.43%	87 79.09%	23 20.91%	8.82
	Total	138 86.79%	21 13.21%	236 88.39%	31 11.61%	184 81.06%	43 18.94%	5.74

TABLE 6.1 *(Concluded)*
Portuguese Population in Seven Major Census Metropolitan Areas (CMA), Single vs Multiple Response
(count and as percentage within gender), 1986–96

CMA		1986		1991		1996		% Change 1986–96 (Multiple Response)
		Single	Multiple	Single	Multiple	Single	Multiple	
Calgary	Female	17 65.38%	9 34.62%	23 74.19%	8 25.81%	25 48.08%	27 51.92%	17.31
	Male	22 68.75%	10 31.25%	25 60.98%	16 39.02%	22 50.00%	22 50.00%	18.75
	Total	39 67.24%	19 32.76%	48 66.67%	24 33.33%	47 48.96%	49 51.04%	18.28
Edmonton	Female	42 76.36%	13 23.64%	76 69.09%	34 30.91%	65 75.58%	21 24.42%	0.78
	Male	48 82.76%	10 17.24%	75 82.42%	16 17.58%	72 74.23%	25 25.77%	8.53
	Total	90 79.65%	23 20.35%	151 75.12%	50 24.88%	137 74.86%	46 25.14%	4.78
Vancouver	Female	96 79.34%	25 20.66%	142 78.89%	38 21.11%	131 56.71%	100 43.29%	22.63
	Male	71 78.89%	19 21.11%	151 71.56%	60 28.44%	128 57.66%	94 42.34%	21.23
	Total	167 79.15%	44 20.85%	293 74.94%	98 25.06%	259 57.17%	194 42.83%	21.97

Source: Based on a 2–3% sample of the Canadian population in Statistics Canada, Public Use Microdata Files (1986, 1991, 1996)

In 1996, in a census sample of seven of the most important urban destinations for Portuguese in Canada, an average of 30 per cent of the Portuguese identified themselves as having multiple ethnic origins (i.e., not just Portuguese, but also Canadian and/or another ethnic origin). This represents a 60 per cent increase from 1986.[2] It is notable, however, that on average, Portuguese women lag behind men in defining themselves in multiple ways. The three cities with the least overall change towards multiple ethnic identity are Edmonton, Winnipeg, and Toronto, whereas the Portuguese in Vancouver have exhibited the most change. In Toronto, the density of the Portuguese immigrant population may play a role in the persistence of a Portuguese ethnic identity. Thus, although Portuguese, especially women, still rely on ethnic identity as a form of resistance to inequity and the lack of access to more broadly based anti-racist, feminist, education and labour-based coalitions, they increasingly define themselves in a heterogeneous way. In the next section of this chapter I analyse another nationalism that affects the lives of Portuguese immigrants, Canadian multiculturalism.

Multiculturalism: The View from the State

The concept of 'diaspora space,' as developed by Brah, is useful in envisaging how the policies and politics of emigration from Portugal and immigration to Canada are intrinsic to the lives of immigrants and to all members of civil society: 'Diaspora space is the intersectionality of diaspora, border and dis/location as a point of confluence of economic, political, cultural and psychic processes ... [and] is "inhabited" not only by those who have migrated and their descendants but equally by those who are constructed and represented as indigenous' (Brah 1996:181). Although immigration and multicultural policies affect everyone in Canada, not simply those defined as immigrants, they are differentially reflected in the everyday gender, class, and race relations of all those located in the nation-state. Thus, although peoples, cultures, and commodities may all share the same space, as Brah points out, regimes of power situate them differently, so that 'the concept of diaspora centres on the *configurations of power which differentiate diasporas internally as well as situate them in relation to one another'* (ibid.:183, her emphasis), empowering some and disempowering others.

Through the case of Portuguese immigration I have tried to demonstrate how multiculturalism policy, in place since the early 1970s, defines cultural pluralism in Canada. Stasiulis describes multiculturalism in Canada as 'wedded, as an afterthought' to the original construct of two founding nations, built upon the ideal of bilingualism and biculturalism, thus limiting public acceptance of those 'cultures and peoples at odds with British and French-Canadian institutions' (1999:198–9). Implicit in multicultural discourse in Canada and elsewhere are underlying principles of cultural homogeneity and the encouragement of a belief that all belong to a culturally and spatially unique community, and participate equally in a democratic political process (Miles 1992: 31). It is in the contradictory context of a multicultural discourse that purports equality and democracy, but is structurally embedded in widespread inequality (Miles 1996), based in Canada on the national subjugation of Quebec and aboriginal peoples, that racism and other inequalities of gender and class persist. In Canada, the romantic ideal of multiculturalism has led to unequal relations and participation in the Canadian state as well as to the outright exclusion of specific groups of immigrants at various historical moments.

The divisive approach inherent in state multiculturalism segregates and isolates workers from one another along ethnic lines, and also dissolves gender, class, and racist divisions into ethnic identity. This discourse sustains the inequities experienced through immigration policies and the marginalization of some members of society to 'the twilight zone in between the liberal and republican constructions of citizenship, where religious, ethnic and sexual minorities are located – outside the national "moral community" but inside the civic nation' (Yuval-Davis 1996:16). In this space, minorities are managed by the state to serve its own interests, which are rarely uniform or coherent, but which to a great extent are those of the political hegemonic forces. Such a process does not occur easily, as Kay Anderson shows in her history of the Chinese in Vancouver, from the early days of their settlement when force was required to subjugate their labour power, to more recent times when British Columbia has become a society of 'European institutional completeness' (K. Anderson 1991:23–4). Anderson describes a continuity of 'the iconic hegemony of [European] white identity' from the mid-1800s when Chinese were defined as 'outsiders' to the present day, when multicultural policies perpetuate 'the myth of a one-character nation' (1991:27), despite a contradictory emphasis on cultural pluralism. Her work demonstrates how the rhetoric of multiculturalism has affected the history of that particular immigrant group, defining them in relation to 'a Canadian society,' as if the latter were a separate and pre-existing entity (1991:218). The mosaic ideology of Canadian multiculturalism in fact reaffirms we-they distinctions that have shaped Canadian immigration policy since its inception (ibid.). Chinese, Italians, Portuguese, and other immigrant groups have been affected by the pluralist politics of multiculturalism that maintain popular beliefs about differences between groups, while simultaneously strengthening exclusionary concepts of a mainstream anglo-European society to which others can contribute. Thus defined, multiculturalism is embedded in an anglo-nationalist agenda that seeks to further its own interests.

As Ng points out, the formation of the Canadian capitalist state can be traced through a history of colonization and immigration policies that have changed over time to suit 'the demands of nation building' (1993:203). As Canada developed from a colony of France and then of England to a nation-state, unequal relations of nation, class, ethnicity, and gender, embedded in particular relations of production and reproduction have gradually crystallized (ibid.). Class, gender, and racial categorizations cross-cut, shape, and define immigration and multicultural policies in cultural, social, and economic ways, on an international as well as national level. Canada's post-World War II immigration and refugee policies have continued to be influenced overwhelmingly by economics and anglo-European nationalism. 'Self-sustaining' is the term that has traditionally been used to define the ideal immigrants and refugees to Canada, and 'absorptive capacity' as the condition for opening the doors (Adelman 1993). Bottomley points out that the tension between the nation-state and forms of ethnicity requires further study. She argues that, although nation-states often are founded on notions of an ethnic collectivity, frequently it is the ethnicity of the dominant group that shapes this nation-state in reference to excluded others and thus, also, in an essentialist way (1997:46). This process is illustrated in the recent state document, *Not Just Numbers: A Canadian Framework for Future Immigration*. Although there is an acknowledgement in this document that 'without immigration and a rising birth rate, the size of the Canadian population will begin to decline in the twenty-first century' (Immigration Legislative Review Advisory Group 1997:1:5), there is no mention of issues of ethnic, gender, class, or other differences and the implications of these for both the settled populations and newcomers to Canada. The document instead makes reference to citizenship as the means to access 'equality of opportunity,' and to legal definitions of 'Canadian values' as expressed by the Supreme Court of Canada in 1986: 'The Court must be guided by the values and principles essential to a free and democratic society ... to name but a few ... accommodation of a wide variety of beliefs, respect for cultural and group identity ...' (ibid. 2:7). These words reiterate the reality of a dominant Anglophone nation to which others can contribute and thus be 'accommodated' and/or 'respected.'

It is assumed in *Not Just Numbers* that citizenship occurs either by birth or by 'choice.' The citizenship definition that is used is derived from the words of Liberal MP Paul Martin Sr. when he introduced the Citizenship Act to the House of Commons in 1946. He defined citizenship in the following way: 'Citizenship means more than the right to vote; more than the right to hold and transfer property; more than the right to move freely under the protection of the state; citizenship is the right to full partnership in the fortunes and in the future of the nation' (ibid. 1:11). Such definitions of citizenship assume that the boundaries of the national collectivity and civil society are the same and unchanging, or 'organically whole,' as feminists have argued (Stasiulis and Yuval-Davis 1995; Yuval-Davis 1991). However, this clearly is not the case for many women, immigrants, refugees, and racial minorities in Canada, who continue to live within the boundaries of civil society, but outside the boundaries of the Canadian nation, and thus do not have the same access to citizenship or citizenship rights as for example, white anglophone middle-class men. There is no indication in *Not Just Numbers* as to how these populations might be brought into 'full partnership in the fortunes and future of the [Canadian] nation,' though there is the assumption that wealthier immigrants are more acceptable. Indeed, without mention or analysis of the difference and diversity in Canadian civil society, or critique of the exclusionary aspects of citizenship, it is unlikely there will be much change in the citizenship status of the already excluded groups, except increasingly to delimit the possibilities of their full participation.

It is generally agreed that in order to understand the unevenness of state practices and their effects, it is important to retain the concept of 'the state'; to analyse it as 'more than mere government' (K. Anderson 1991:24); and to see it as being organized around the control and enforcement of privilege (Stasiulis and Yuval-Davis 1995:17). I concur with Yuval-Davis and Anthias that the state can be conceptualized as a particular set 'of institutions and relations which are centrally organized around the intentionality of control with a given apparatus of enforcement at its command' (1989:5). Similarly, I agree that civil society can be conceptualized as 'a social space, networks, institutions, and social relations, including families, households, voluntary associations, the production of signs and symbols, and in some definitions, production relations' (Stasiulis and Yuval-Davis 1995:17). What is of importance to the study of Portuguese here, is to understand the ways in which the history, structure, and social relations of civil society are entwined with or, to borrow Brah's terminology, are 'immanent in' state politics and practices that have affected their settlement in quite specific ways. These nationalist and state multicultural politics and practices are interrelated with global restructuring, a relationship that has not been adequately addressed.

Mouffe argued in 1979 that '"the national question" is one of the areas where marxist theory is most seriously lacking and it is urgent, today more than ever, that the question be posed correctly' (Mouffe 1979:9). Since Mouffe made this statement in the late 1970s, research has begun to bring marxism to bear on questions of gendered forms of nationalism vis-à-vis ethnicity (McAll 1990; K. Anderson 1991; Jayawardena 1986; Brah 1996; Gilroy 1993, etc.) and globalization (Basch et al. 1994; Bakan and Stasiulis 1997, etc.). But more work needs to be done to understand the relationships between nationalism and globalization and the gendered relationships inherent to each of these.

Global Inequalities

> The new elements of globalization have created growing levels of social disparities and heightened gender inequality. The economic growth miracle ... is built on the exploitation of women's labour. (Gita Sen, NGO Forum on Women, August 1995, Hairou, China)

The international non-governmental forum in Beijing in 1995 clearly defined economic globalization as one of the most serious threats to women's well-being worldwide. The deleterious effects of globalization, as voiced by Sen, were described also by other speakers as being experienced by women throughout the world, from refugee camps to factories and offices. In this book I have attempted to understand how this process affects Portuguese immigrant women by analysing how the politics of multiculturalism and citizenship, combined with labour-market-oriented immigration policies create gender, class, and ethnic divisions.

Citizenship, similar to the existence of a world-view of 'middle class-lessness,' that Livingstone and Mangan describe as a 'faded memory' of a 1960s' expansionist Canada (1996:1), is generally regarded as something accessible to all and as an ideal construct, 'rather than a lived reality' (Stasiulis and Bakan 1997: 117). Following Thompson, who writes that 'Class is defined by men as they live their own history ...' (1963:11), Stasiulis and Bakan draw a parallel between class and citizenship, the latter which exists like class 'specifically, historically, and changes continually as relationships are negotiated and re-negotiated in variable national and international conditions' (1997:118). They add that 'citizenship and non-citizenship, like conflicting classes, emerge simultaneously' (ibid.). They describe the relationship between class, gender, and race/ethnicity and citizenship as follows: '[Citizenship] is a process which renders legal and legitimate discriminations based on whether individuals embody capital (e.g., as transnational capitalists benefiting from wealth creation in the NICs) or poverty (e.g., of the majority of those living in developing nations), as well as the dominant race/ethnicity and gender' (ibid.:119).[3]

Likewise, Bhabha describes the 'defining characteristic of the modern state' as being 'control over which non-citizens can have access to the territory' (J. Bhabha 1996:6). Thus, in the same way that access/ownership of property is associated with privileged class position, so too, access to certain territories is associated with citizenship status. One of the ways class is expressed is through citizenship practices.

It is this relationship, between class, citizenship, and globalization processes that I wish to pursue here. Two positions obfuscate critiques of citizenship and nation-state boundaries. On the one hand, it is argued that increasingly open borders will facilitate the entry and citizenship rights of the kinds of immigrants who might otherwise experience restrictions (e.g., refugees, unskilled labour migrants, and so-called dependent immigrants, particularly women). On the other hand, policies of boundary liberalization are regarded also as playing into the hands of predatory global capitalists, whose goals may be viewed as threatening the industry, cultural, and social identity of workers and citizens of Canada. The latter argument sometimes is used in liberal and left analyses to insist on the limitation of the entry of immigrants and their access to various kinds of citizenship. Immigrant workers, for example, often have been regarded as a threat to jobs and wages by indigenous workers who may consider themselves, as citizens, to be a superior economic and cultural force, or at least to be more deserving of employment and state resources. Along with a capitalist need to control labour, this has translated into state concerns about 'social order,' leading to policies that are meant to control and manage the 'disorder' caused by the flow of immigrants into the nation-state (Miles and Satzewich 1990:352). Canadian immigration policy that has traditionally focused on the skills of immigrants, and thus their economic contribution, exemplifies this approach. Reflecting immigration policy, this approach is demonstrated both by European Union policies and by NAFTA: capitalists always define the flow of labour in terms of its profitability, rather than as a threat to the jobs of nationals.

Therefore, to focus the argument on whether, or the extent to which, borders should be open or closed, in the context of an increasingly transnational environment (as exemplified by exchanges of remittances and certain categories of labour, as well as return migrations), is simplistic. Although nation-state boundaries and borders sometimes may assist in the protection of indigenous workers, it is also the case that the place called home is not always a haven, depending on the home site and historical period in which one lives and works (i.e., populations affected and trapped by war, apartheid, slavery, gender persecution, environmental disasters) (Giles and Hyndman, forthcoming). It is important to understand the complex ways in which capital and citizenship as processes are intertwined, contributing to class, gender, and race/ethnicity formations nationally and internationally. State multiculturalism and immigration policy are part of regional and international economic and trade relationships and must be understood as such. However, international trade relations historically have not been considered part of immigration policy, and thus negotiations toward such agreements have not normally included safeguards for the well-being of immigrant workers.[4] Workplace protections and access to adequate services should be assured to all workers and their families, whether indigenous or immigrant. Indeed, international human rights fora should sanction countries whose immigration policies do not provide such protections and services. However, international human rights instruments either do not address this issue or do so in a limited or nominal way. Examples of infractions of citizenship/human rights are repeated in various ways among immigrant minority groups in Canada and elsewhere, as for example, this country's history of requesting bulk orders of Portuguese male labourers to build the Canadian railway lines, the lack of protection experienced by Portuguese domestic service and industrial workers, the chronically limited access of Portuguese immigrant women to language training classes, and the streaming of Portuguese children.

Kearney argues that, in practice, immigration policy, is actually 'disguised labour policy' (Cockcroft, 1986 cited in Kearney 1991:71), and as such is based on a separation of productive and reproductive spaces. His reflections on immigration practices in the United States have implications for our understanding of Canada's immigration/labour policies in an era of free trade harmonization and transnationalism: 'Capitalism in general effects the alienation of labor from its owner, but immigration policy can be seen as a means to achieve a form of this alienation that increases greatly in the age of transnationalism, namely the spatial separation of the site of the purchase and expenditure of labor from the sites of its reproduction, such that the locus of production and reproduction lie in two different national spaces' (1991:58–9).

Ideally, temporary migrant workers fulfil this goal. Notably, since the 1970s, labour migration strategy in Canada has tended increasingly to resort to temporary employment as opposed to permanent immigration in order to address labour shortages (Arat-Koc 1990: 93). One of the effects of this trend is that the designation of a group of workers as temporary contributes to a desensitized attitude towards their working and living conditions by the general, settled population (ibid.). The increasing demand for skilled, English and/or French speaking labour in Canada and the lack of educational opportunities for immigrants who have been accepted into Canada demonstrates this policy; i.e., that immigrants either will have received their education at the expense of another country or do without. As I have demonstrated in this book, Portuguese immigrant women are an example of a group who have been relatively unsuccessful at accessing even basic language and skills education in Canada.

Peterson points out that a global world system, premised on capitalist accumulation, raises serious questions about 'the nature of governance, the meaning of democratization, and the location of political accountability' (1996:13). In this global context, Stasiulis and Jhappan describe a 'backlash' against the 'third world origins of most immigrant newcomers,' whose arrival is perceived as an economic and cultural threat by the 'white settler colony' (1995:124). This siege mentality becomes more obvious once the cloak of multiculturalism is lifted. As the context of economic globalization comes into focus, the guise of multiculturalism begins to fall away, and immigrants can be distinguished as workers and not simply members of particular ethnic groups. Behind a countenance of pluralism, class relations and citizenship negotiations are continually being played out. Exclusionary immigration policies are one of the means of enacting state multicultural discourse in Canada. As Pateman (1989) points out in her discussion of citizenship and gender – that I extend to an analysis of immigration and gender – women in particular are social exiles, caught in a contradictory situation in which they contribute in the productive sphere, but are excluded from full citizenship.

Community, Contradictions, and Struggle

This brings us to questions about communities of resistance, and how these might be defined in a multi-ethnic nation. Here I refer to the parts played by gender, race, and class in the construction of communities of resistance. In order to immigrate here, Portuguese workers must enter a realm of power relations that is organized along two nations (English and French) or three nations (English, French, and Aboriginal) principles.[5] Despite the pluralistic discourse of multicultural policy, this framework excludes other groups, such as the Portuguese, affecting not only their attachment to and struggle in creating a Portuguese community, but also gendered forms of resistance in the face of nationalist and multicultural policies.

How have struggles concerned with Portuguese ethnic identity intersected with the broader feminist movements in Canada and in Portugal? To what extent have these relationships/coalitions been difficult to attain or indeed, undesirable? Paralleling these processes is the history of women's movements in Canada and, in particular, the historical position of ethnic minority feminists in these movements. Stasiulis argues there is a trend towards anti-racist pluralism in women's movements in this country that is 'best exemplified by the structural changes undertaken and issues championed by NAC (the National Action Committee on the Status of Women), the largest umbrella group for feminist organizations in Canada' (1999:207). However, she argues that '[the] tendency to democratic pluralism [in NAC] has occurred without resolving the contradictions inherent in the historically structured positions of inequality of women's racial/ethnic communities, the relative merits of their claims for self-determination and entitlements, and the possibly negative implications for women from other communities of the pursuit of feminist-nationalist projects' (ibid.:208). Accordingly, Stasiulis raises a question about the potential for creating solidarity among women when their attachments to their respective ethnonational communities are 'politically foregrounded' (ibid.:210). These ideas raise concerns for feminist politics. Arguing about the importance of an anti-essentialist approach, Mouffe writes: 'It is therefore impossible to speak of the social agent as if we were dealing with a unified homogeneous entity. We have rather to approach it as a plurality, dependent on the various subject positions through which it is constituted within various discursive formations' (1992:372).

The challenge is to retain plurality and broaden feminist political projects at one and the same time. Anthias, Bannerji, Brah, and Yuval-Davis take Mouffe's approach further, incorporating an ethnic/race analysis into Mouffe's focus on gender, as well as critiquing the lack of positioning of some feminist theorizing on difference. Taking an anti-essentialist view, Yuval-Davis states that community is not a 'given, natural unit to which one can either belong or not' (1996:5). Rather, as she and Anthias argue, communities are 'ideological and material constructions, whose boundaries, structures and norms are the result of constant processes of struggle and negotiations, or more general social developments' (Yuval-Davis 1996:5; Anthias and Yuval-Davis 1992). Thus, 'political mobilizations' must take into account that different collectivities/communities are positioned differently in relation to the state (Yuval-Davis 1996:5).

Also relevant are Brah's ideas (discussed earlier in this chapter) concerning the ways in which regimes of power situate various groups differently, both internally and in relation to one another (1996:183), empowering some and disempowering others. The response of feminist women to inequalities either within their group or in relation to other groups is often expressed in nationalist or ethnic minority claims, which raise questions about 'the extent to which feminist projects are complementary or contradictory' (Stasiulis 1999:184). Stasiulis argues that an acceptance of pluralism has been crucial to women's movements in Canada as they have struggled, with some success, for the extension of rights to marginalized groups of women. However, this struggle does not address the complicated power dynamics of 'relational positionality,' which, in addition to a recognition of plurality, 'more importantly,' addresses 'the *positionality* of different nationalisms, racisms, ethnocultural movements, and feminisms *in relation to one another*' (ibid.:183).

An understanding of the relational positionality of women in Canada (not only ethnic/racial, but also class, etc.) should be a first step in the development of a feminist politics that attends to the concerns of immigrant women and their descendants.[6] Multiculturalist and Canadian nationalist ideologies and policies hinder our progress towards the development and endurance of a unified women's movement in this country. Part of this first step is a theorization of feminism, central to which is a comparative analysis of feminist organizing, criticism, and self-reflection (Alexander and Mohanty 1997:xx), and a rejection of all forms of nationalism.

I have argued elsewhere that comparative research potentially represents an activist approach that can work toward the elimination of inequality and oppression (Giles 1999). State multicultural policy obstructs comparative work and is vulnerable to comparisons that are characterized by a static essentialism which denies difference and divergent histories of domination and dominance. Hyndman, like Alexander and Mohanty, argues for 'transnational feminist practices: political action which conceives of differences as linked, if unequal, and which upsets commonplace markers of social, cultural and political identity' (1996:17). She regards feminist transnational practices as challenging purely locational (and, I would add, nationalist) politics, and as engaging and connecting rather than distinguishing and distancing people of different locations (see also Grewal and Kaplan 1994).

This approach is related to what Bottomley, drawing on Bourdieu, describes as the 'practice' of multiethnic pluralistic openness to difference. She argues that the success of multiculturalism – in the best sense of this phenomenon – is due to a 'logic of practice' (Bottomley 1997:47). This relates to Bourdieu's definition of social groups as identifying in a 'polythetic' way, and thus 'sustaining a multiplicity of contradictory meanings,' while 'practising' everyday life together (ibid.). In addition, class 'habituses' are continuously changing structures wherein individuals constantly re/create themselves in the historical and contradictory images of the collective group or class, while a 'practical logic' operates across this heterogeneity (Livingstone and Mangan 1999:27; Robbins 1991:112). It is this notion of 'practice' that is central to my analysis of multicultural, immigration, and citizenship practices in Canada. As well, Gramscian theories of hegemony offer a pivotal perspective of the nation-state – from the other face of multiculturalism – a standpoint circumscribed by definitions of citizenship and immigration policy. As McClintock argues, 'All nations depend on powerful constructions of gender. Despite many nationalists' ideological investment in the idea of popular *unity*, nations have historically amounted to the sanctioned institutionalization of gender *difference'* (1993:62). Gender, race, and class relations are associated with nationalisms and shape immigration policies and global ways of living and working. This is the reason why so little attention has been paid to the lives and work of the immigrant women who formed the majority of immigrant workers from Portugal during the height of the Portuguese migration to Canada.

Notes

1: Introduction

1 A debate on this issue between Howard-Hassman (1999, 2000) and Abu-Laban and Stasiulis (2000) is contained in *Canadian Public Policy* (volumes 25 and 26).
2 All the names of interviewees in this book are pseudonyms.
3 My research also includes interviews with 20 working-class, anglophone, Canadian-born women. These interviews have been useful for comparative purposes, and are included in the analysis of education in Chapter Five.
4 There is little or no agreement among those working on intergenerational studies on immigrants about how to define various generational groups, or whether such a division is useful at all. Noivo (1997:139), for example, recognizes the variety of ways that 'generations' have been defined sociologically and adapts these definitions to her understanding of the Portuguese who live in and around Montreal. She 'ranks' family members generationally, using normative principles of kinship descent, and grouping by 'cohorts' (ibid.). The entry point to my field study is linked to my earlier research on the relationship between language fluency and equity issues (Giles 1988). Thus, to begin with, interviewees were divided into English-speakers and non-English speakers. The data from these interviews revealed a relationship between gender, language fluency, levels of education, employment, and age at entry. From these data, two principle groupings or generations were revealed. Although there may be some members of the Portuguese community who do not fit this heuristic framework, it remains a useful analytical tool.
5 Emigration was restricted during the years of the dictatorship in Portugal

(the early 1930s to 1974); thus, many Portuguese left without government permission.

6 In the case of one Portuguese woman in this study, Brazil was the first place to which she immigrated before moving to Canada.

2: Where Have All the Women Gone?

1 See also the following unpublished theses: Aguiar 1994; Grosner 1991; Januário 1988.

2 My use of the term 'discourse' is similar to that of Stasiulis and Yuval-Davis, who write that collectivities become labelled as ethnic, racial, and nationalist by various agents and/or historical circumstances, and what varies are the 'distinctive discourses and projects of ethnicity, racism and nationalism' (1995:20). Likewise, I use the term 'discourse' to refer to social practices, forms of subjectivity (i.e., who you define as 'we' and 'they') and power relations. Not all discourses carry equal weight or power: some justify the status quo and others challenge the status quo. In any society, one discourse is dominant and reflects the particular values and class, gender, and racial interests of that society.

3 The results of the 1997 Immigration Legislative Review, as detailed in *Not Just Numbers* (Immigration Legislative Review Advisory Group 1997), were controversial and led to a revised document, *Building on a Strong Foundation for the 21st Century: New Directions for Immigration and Refugee Policy and Legislation* (Citizenship and Immigration Canada 1998).

4 In 1996 the Minister of Citizenship and Immigration proposed the elimination of automatic citizenship for children born in Canada to non-residents and refugees. This initiative would have left some children stateless, and was strongly opposed by many non-governmental immigrant groups. As a result, the government proposal has been withdrawn, at least temporarily (Treviranus 1999).

5 Hyndman argues that *Not Just Numbers* proposes 'very gendered streams of masculine expertise and feminized need' (1999:10).

6 Domestic workers from the Caribbean also arrived during this period in what were called 'batch[es] of girls' (Harzig 1999:136)

7 These workers travelled to a variety of locations and jobs in Canada. Some, for example, went as far as the west coast of Canada and into the interior of British Columbia, where they worked in sawmills, pulp and paper mills, aluminum smelters, and fish canneries (Anderson and Higgs 1976:102–3).

8 My objective definitions of class draw principally on the works of Wright and Livingstone Wright (1978, 1985), who has developed one of the most

influential descriptions of contemporary class structure, argues that certain workers may be defined as exploited because they do not own the means of production, but they are opposed to proletarians because they have 'effective control of organization and skill assets' (Wright 1985:87). Livingston proposes a class scheme that is similar to that of Wright, insofar as 'the major criteria are ownership of the means of production and exercise of control over the labour process ...' (Livingston and Mangan 1996:23). Livingston's class of 'rentier capitalists' is akin to my definition of 'upper class,' and could also include some of my 'middle class.' His 'petty-bourgeoisie' is akin to my 'middle class.' His 'industrial' and 'non-industrial' working-group and those located in 'subemployment' most closely reflect my use of the term 'working class.'

However, Portuguese immigrant women and their daughters express a good deal of class heterogeneity in their everyday lives as they travel between their household, community, and wage workplace, in addition to the two countries in which they claim (or have the potential to claim) citizenship. They demonstrate the fractured and uneven development of class processes vis-à-vis immigrants and in general. The work of Gramsci and, in particular, Bourdieu has helped me to understand these more processual aspects of class. Bourdieu describes class 'habituses' as continuously changing structures in which individuals constantly re/create themselves in the historical and contradictory images of the collective group or class, while a 'practical logic' operates across this heterogeneity (Livingstone and Mangan:27, Robbins:112). In other words, Bourdieu defines social groups as identifying in a 'polythetic' (many positions) way and thus 'sustaining a multiplicity of contradictory meanings,' while at the same time 'practising' everyday life together (Bottomley 1997:47).

9 Not until the early to mid-1990s did another European group of immigrants – the Poles – enter Canada in significant numbers. However, in the period 1991–6, at the height of their immigration, they represented 3.6 per cent of the total migration, well below the migration from Hong Kong which constituted the highest, 10.5 per cent of the total number during that period (Statistics Canada 1996:4–5). Portuguese formed the largest group of immigrants to enter Toronto in the period from 1967 to 1977, with slightly more Portuguese women than men immigrating to Toronto (Statistics Canada 1986).

10 Portugal is now both a labour-exporting and labour-importing country, with immigrants from its former colonies, Brazil, Timor, Macau, Mozambique, Guinea-Bissau, São Tomé, Cabo Verde, and Angola, arriving on its shores in search of wages and other livelihood resources (Rocha-Trindade 1993:278, 2000).

11 One of the few pieces of research that explore the lives of Azorean women and regional differences is Grosner's (1991) unpublished M.A. thesis on Azorean women in London, Ontario. Melo's recent unpublished M.A. thesis also makes an important contribution to our knowledge of Azorean returnees (1997).
12 See also Januário and Marujo's findings (2000).
13 Baganha (1998:199) writes that most of the returnees to Portugal have been male (71 per cent of the total).
14 Smith also states that, for the majority of women she interviewed in the U.S., the family moved to locations where women had kin and men had none (Ibid.:80).
15 The absence of adequate and relevant language training, education, and skills training for such a significant number of immigrant women and men wage workers has grave consequences for the workers themselves and for the Canadian economy.

3: Culture, Politics, and Resistance in the Household

1 Sections of this chapter were previously published in Giles (1997).
2 See for example, Bottomley 1991, Lamphere 1987, and *The Special Issue of The International Migration Review: The New Second-Generation*, edited by Alejandro Portes (1994).
3 During wars waged by the Angolan and Mozambican liberation movements against the Portuguese, it was not uncommon for Portuguese households with young sons to migrate to Canada or elsewhere. This type of migration contradicts the view that southern European migration is solely economically based, and underlines the importance of examining the relationship of migrations to global issues, including political issues.
4 Although women may own land, their access to the resources of the land in many parts of Portugal is related to their ability to marry, and marriage is viewed as necessary for the formation of a household (de Pina-Cabral 1984). However, landless women who are less likely to find husbands in northwestern rural Portugal sometimes challenge the naturalized ideologies of their roles, and emigrate to find jobs and/or marriage partners elsewhere in Portugal, or in other countries (Giles and Januario 1987).

4: Working Lives

1 The Statistics Canada categories, 'Portuguese foreign-born' and 'Portuguese Canadian-born' (based on ethnic origin/place of birth) are similar

to the categories I have used in my research for this book, i.e., 'first-generation' and 'second-generation' Portuguese. Although these terms are not identical, they do overlap in significant ways: 'Portuguese foreign-born' is analogous to my category 'first generation' insofar as it includes those born and educated in Portugal. However, it differs from my 'first generation' since it includes those born in Portugal and educated in Canada. 'Portuguese Canadian-born' is analogous to my category 'second generation,' except that it does not include those born in Portugal and educated in Canada.

2 See previous note 1.

3 This is the date of the social democratic revolution in Portugal.

4 Bourdieu's comments regarding the ways in which people identify 'polythetically,' while 'practising' everyday life together are relevant in this regard, and are discussed further in Chapter Six.

5 Januario (1988), in her research in Montreal, also refers to the effects of paternalism on Portuguese workers.

6 Portuguese immigrant women in Canada, along with Greek and Italian women, are among the groups most likely not to be able to converse in English or French (Boyd 1990).

5: Ethnoculturalism, Education, and Restructuring

1 It is well known, however, that some members of ethnic-nationalist groups living in Canada do support nationalist struggles in their countries of origin with money and other resources accumulated in this country.

2 Ana Cristina Costa is the author of the 1995 report: *Conference Report: 'From Coast to Coast: A Community in Transition,'* Portuguese National Conference, University of Ottawa, March, 1993. I do not reference the names of the individual speakers at any of these three conferences.

3 The title of the conference is taken from a well-known 1976 book by Grace Anderson and David Higgs, *A Future to Inherit: Portuguese Communities in Canada.* As described in the Introduction to this book, it is part of a series mandated by the federal government in response to Book IV of the *Report on the Royal Commission on Bilingualism and Biculturalism* (1969) that dealt with ethnic groups other than the British, French, and Native peoples.

4 João Rolo, is the author of the 1998: *Conference Report: 'It's Time to Inherit the Future': Portuguese Canadian National Youth Conference,* 23–5 May 1997. I do not reference the names of the individual speakers at any of these three conferences.

5 In Chapter Six, I argue that Portuguese are identifying increasingly in a

multiple way (as Portuguese and Canadian or another ethnic origin).

6 Kay Anderson describes 'Chineseness' as 'a politically effective counter-ideology' under Canada's policy of multiculturalism. She gives an example of how neighbourhood upgrading schemes, refurbishing the Chinatown district 'in the image of Western constructs of the East, has been used by Chinatown's merchants, to their own advantage' (Anderson 1991:27).

7 In Portugal, access to education is more readily available than in the past, and in 1990, only 2 per cent of women aged 15 to 25 years old were illiterate (Seager 1997:85). However, older women in Portugal are still unable to freely access education: 32 per cent of women aged 25 years and older are illiterate (Seager 1997:85). Although worldwide the enrolment of girls in school has increased faster than it has for boys, they are still educated in fewer numbers than boys (Seager 1997:123).

8 As I describe more fully in note 1 in Chapter Four, the Statistics Canada categories, 'Portuguese foreign-born' and 'Portuguese Canadian-born' are similar to the categories 'first generation' and 'second generation' used in my qualitative research for this book.

9 Some of these Canadian-born women were located through their contact with a university bridging program. Thus, their attendance at college and university is greater than that for the general population of Canadian-born, anglophone, working-class women. The Statistics Canada data in Table 5.1 demonstrate that in 1991 (at the time my research was carried out) 43 per cent of all Canadian-born women (excluding Portuguese-born women) had achieved a college or university degree.

6: Conclusion – Nationalisms and Differences

1 Children are often pulled into nationalist struggles, as evidenced by the highly publicized story of Elian Gonzalez, the Cuban boy who lost both his mother and step-father at sea off the coast of Florida in their attempt to enter the United States. He was claimed by his anti-Castro relatives in Florida, his father in Cuba, the Cuban state and, in a rather ambivalent way, the United States.

2 Research by Meintel in Montreal confirms the importance of plural identities to the children of immigrants who regard these 'mixed' identities as 'a source of enrichment rather than a source of inner conflict'(forthcoming: 1). Indeed, these youth lay claim to all their 'ethnically specific identities' which they use selectively, depending on the context and without negating any of their other identities (ibid.).

3 Gibson-Graham refers to 'place' as increasingly being 'seen as an important constituent of actual classes' (1997:50). Thus immigrants from some regions of the world, i.e., developing nations, are defined as members of an underclass, with a corresponding definition of citizenship.

4 This is now changing as human rights activists challenge the World Trade Organization, the International Monetary Fund, and other international and national financial institutions over the relationship between trade agreements and labour conditions. However, as Hoerder points out, 'illegal' migrants, or those without acceptable documentation, are vulnerable to the worst conditions of global economic exploitation, and normally are the last to be recognized by human rights policies (Hoerder 2000:113).

5 NAC adopted a 'three nations' position in the debates associated with the 1992 Charlottetown Accord (Stasiulis 1999:206; Vickers et al. 1993:9). As Stasiulis points out, this formulation failed to address *relations of power and/or colonialism* among ethnic/racial collectivities,' and 'it also does not speak to the representation and interests of women of colour, immigrant and refugee women who did not see themselves reflected in discourses of "two nations" or "three nations"' (Stasiulis 1999:206).

6 Other 'pluralistic and diversified practice[s] of citizenship' that challenge the restrictions of national borders and the negative effects of globalization on women and are concerned with women's human rights are being developed by those concerned with spatial formations and, in particular, cities (Wekerle 2000).

References

Abreu-Ferreira, Darlene. 1995–6. The Portuguese in Newfoundland: Documentary Evidence Examined. *Portuguese Studies Review* 4, 2 (Fall–Winter) 11–33.

Abu-Laban, Yasmeen, and Daiva Stasiulis. 2000. Constructing 'Ethnic Canadians': The Implications for Public Policy and Inclusive Citizenship. *Canadian Public Policy* 26, 4: 477–87.

Adelman, Howard. 1993. Categories of Refugees. Paper presented at the Conference on Immigration to Australia and Canada. Carleton: Melbourne University Press.

Aguiar, Maria Margarida M. 1994. The School and Immigration Histories of Women from the Islands of São Miguel in the Azores Region of Portugal. M.A. thesis, Department of Education, University of Toronto.

Alexander, M. Jacqui, and Chandra Talpade Mohanty. 1997. Introduction: Genealogies, Legacies, Movements. In *Feminist Genealogies, Colonial Legacies, Democratic Futures*, ed. M. Jacqui Alexander and Chandra Talpade Mohanty, xiii–xlii. New York: Routledge.

Alpalhao, J. Antonio, and Victor M.P. Da Rosa. 1980. *A Minority in a Changing Society: The Portuguese Communities of Quebec*. Ottawa: University of Ottawa Press.

Anderson, Benedict. 1991. *Imagined Communities: Reflections on the Origin and Spread of Nationalism*. Revised Edition. New York: Verso.

Anderson, Grace. 1974. *Networks of Contact: The Portuguese in Toronto*. Waterloo: Wilfrid Laurier University Press.

Anderson, Grace, and David Higgs. 1976. *A Future to Inherit: Portuguese Communities in Canada*. Toronto: McClelland and Stewart.

Anderson, Grace, and J. Campbell Davis. 1990. Portuguese Immigrant Women in Canada. In *Portuguese Migration in Global Perspective*, ed. D. Higgs, 136–44. Toronto: Multicultural History Society of Ontario.

Anderson, Kay J. 1991. *Vancouver's Chinatown: Racial Discourse in Canada, 1875–1980*. Kingston and Montreal: McGill-Queen's University Press.

Anthias, Floya, and Nira Yuval-Davis, in association with Harriet Cain. 1992. *Racialized Boundaries*. New York and London: Routledge.

Anthropological Quarterly 1976. Department of Anthropology. Special Issue on Women and Migration. The Catholic University of America. Press. Washington. D.C. Volume 49, No 1.

Arat-Koc, Sedef. 1990. Importing Housewives: Non-Citizen Domestic Workers and the Crisis of the Domestic Sphere in Canada. *Through the Kitchen Window: The Politics of Home and Family*. 2nd enlarged edition, ed. Meg Luxton, Harriet Rosenberg, and Sedef Arat-Koc, 81–103. Toronto: Garamond Press.

– 1997. From 'Mothers of the Nation' to Migrant Workers. In *Not One of the Family: Foreign Domestic Workers in Canada*, ed. Abigail B. Bakan and Daiva Stasiulis, 53–80. Toronto: University of Toronto Press.

– 1999a. Gender and Race in 'Non-Discriminatory' Immigration Policies in Canada. In *Scratching the Surface: Canadian Anti-Racist Feminist Thought*, ed. Enakshi Dua & Angela Robertson, 207–33. Toronto: Women's Press.

– 1999b. NAC's Response to the Immigration Legislative Review Report: 'Not Just Numbers: A Canadian Framework for Future Immigration.' *Canadian Women's Studies Journal* 19, 3: 18–23.

Arat-Koc, Sedef, and Wenona Giles. 1994. Introduction. *Maid in the Market: Women's Paid Domestic Labour*, ed. Wenona Giles and Sedef Arat-Koc, 1–12. Halifax: Fernwood Publishing.

Baganha, Maria Ioannis B. 1998. Portuguese Emigration after World War II. In *Modern Portugal*, ed. Antonio Costa Pinto, 189–203. Palo Alto: The Society for the Promotion of Science and Scholarship.

Bakan, Abigail B., and Daiva Stasiulis. 1997. Foreign Domestic Worker Policy in Canada and the Social Boundaries of Modern Citizenship. In *Not One of the Family: Foreign Domestic Workers in Canada*, ed. Abigail B. Bakan and Daiva Stasiulis, 29–52. Toronto: University of Toronto Press.

Bannerji, Himani. 1995. *Thinking Through: Essays on Feminism, Marxism and Anti-Racism*. Toronto: Women's Press.

Barrett, Michèle. 1991. *The Politics of Truth: From Marx to Foucault*. Oxford: Polity Press.

Basch, Linda, Nina Glick Schiller, and Cristina Szanton-Blanc. 1994. *Nations Unbound: Transnational Projects and the Deterritorialized Nation-State*. New York: Gordon and Breach.

Bhabha, Jacqueline. 1996. Embodied Rights: Gender Persecution, State Sovereignty and Refugees. *Public Culture*, no. 9: 3–32.

Bhattacharjee, Anannya. 1997. The Public/Private Mirage: Mapping Homes and Undomesticating Violence Work in the South Asian Immigrant Community. In *Feminist Genealogies, Colonial Legacies, Democratic Futures*, ed. M.J. Alexander and C.T. Mohanty, 308–29. New York: Routledge.

Bodnar, John. 1980. Immigration, Kinship, and the Rise of Working Class Realism in Industrial America. *Journal of Social History* 14: 45–65.

Borreicho, Ana, and Antonia Ferreira. 1992. 'A Tradition of Strength and Courage.' *Toronto Star*, G7.

Bottomley, Gill. 1991. Representing the 'Second Generation': Subjects, Objects and Ways of Knowing. In *Intersexions: Gender/Class/Culture/Ethnicity*, ed. Gill Bottomley, Marie de Lepervanche, and Jeannie Martin, 92–109. Sydney: Allen and Unwin.

– 1995a. Living across Difference: Connecting Gender, Ethnicity, Class and Ageing in Australia. Paper presented at the Workshop on the Political Economy of Marriage and the Family, York University, Canada. 30 October 1995.

– 1995b. Women and Families in the Migration Process. Paper presented at the Workshop on the Political Economy of Marriage and the Family, York University, Canada. 1 November 1995.

– 1997. Identification: Ethnicity, Gender and Culture. *Journal of Intercultural Studies* 18, 1: 41–8.

Boyd, Monica. 1975. The Status of Immigrant Women in Canada. *Canadian Review of Sociology and Anthropology* 12: 406–16.

– 1990. Immigrant Women: Language, Socioeconomic Inequalities and Policy Issues. In *Ethnic Demography, Canadian Immigrant, Racial and Cultural Variations*, ed. S.S. Halli, F. Trovato, and L. Dreidger, 275–93. Ottawa: Carleton University Press.

– 1992. Gender, Visible Minority and Immigrant Earnings Inequality: Reassessing an Employment Equity Premise. In *Deconstructing a Nation: Immigration, Multiculturalism and Racism in the 1990s Canada*, ed. V. Satzewich, 279–321. Toronto: Fernwood Press.

Brah, Avtar. 1996. *Cartographies of Diaspora*. London: Routledge.

Brettell, Caroline. 1986. *Men Who Migrate, Women Who Wait: Population and History in a Portuguese Parish*. Princeton: Princeton University Press.

Brunt, Rosalind. 1989. The Politics of Identity. In *New Times: The Changing Face of Politics in the 1990s*, ed. S. Hall and M. Jacques, 150–9. London: Lawrence and Wishart.

Butler, Judith. 1990. *Gender Trouble: Feminism and the Subversion of Identity*. London and New York: Routledge.

Castells, Manuel. 1979. *City, Class and Power*. New York: St Martin's Press.

– 1983. *The City and the Grassroots: A Cross Cultural Theory of Urban Social Movements*. Berkeley: University of California Press.

Canada. 1969. *Report of the Royal Commission on Bilingualism and Biculturalism*. Ottawa: Queen's Printer.

Canadian Heritage Multiculturalism. 1998. Ethnic Identity Reinforces Attachment to Canada. Vol. 1. 21 May 1998. Http://www.pch.gc.ca/multi/evidence/series1.htm.

Chaney, Rick. 1986. *Regional Emigration and Remittances in Developing Countries: The Portuguese Experience*. New York: Praeger.

Citizenship and Immigration. 1996. *A Profile of Immigrants from Portugal in Canada*. Ottawa:

Citizenship and Immigration Canada (CIC). 1998. *Building on a Strong Foundation for the Twenty-First Century: New Directions for Immigration and Refugee Policy and Legislation*. Ottawa: Minister of Public Works and Government Services Canada.

Cockcroft, J.D. 1986. *Outlaws in the Promised Land: Mexican immigration Workers and America's Future*. New York: Grove Press.

Cole, Sally. 1990. Cod, God, Country, and Family: The Portuguese Newfoundland Cod Fishery. *Maritime Anthropological Studies* 3, 1: 1–29.

– 1991. *Women of the Praia: Work and Lives in a Portuguese Coastal Community*. Princeton: Princeton University Press.

– 1998. Reconstituting Households, Retelling Culture: Emigration and Portuguese Fisheries Workers. In *Transgressing Borders: Critical Perspectives on Gender, Household and Culture*, ed. Suzan Ilcan and Lynne Phillips, 75–92. Westport, Connecticut, and London. Bergin and Garvey.

Costa, Ana Cristina. 1995. *Conference Report. From Coast to Coast: A Community in Transition*. Portuguese National Conference, March 1993. Ottawa: University of Ottawa.

Das Gupta, Tania. 1999. The Politics of Multiculturalism: Immigrant Women and the Canadian State. In *Scratching the Surface: Canadian Anti-Racist Feminist Thought*, ed. Enakshi Dua & Angela Robertson, 187–205. Toronto: Women's Press.

de Pina-Cabral, João. 1984. Female Power and the Inequality of Wealth and Motherhood in Northwestern Portugal. *Women and Property, Women as Property*, ed. R. Hirschon, 75–91. Kent: Croom Helm Ltd. Beckenham.

– 1986. *Sons of Adam. Daughters of Eve*. Oxford: Clarendon Press.

Department of Citizenship and Immigration. *Annual Reports*. 1950–65. Ottawa. Queen's Printer.

Departments of Citizenship and Immigration, Manpower and Immigration, and Employment and Immigration. 1962–82. *Immigration Statistics*. Ottawa: Minister of Supply and Services.

Department of Manpower and Immigration. 1975. *A Report of the Canadian*

Immigration and Population Study. Vol. 2. *The Immigration Program.* Ottawa: Minister of Supply and Services.

di Leonardo, Micaela. 1991. *Gender at the Crossroads of Knowledge: Feminist Anthropology in the Postmodern Era.* Berkeley and Los Angeles: University of California Press.

Dorais, Louis-Jacques, Lois Foster, and David Stockley. 1994. Multiculturalism and Integration. In *Immigration and Refugee Policy: Australia and Canada Compared*, ed. H. Adelman, A. Borowski, M. Burstein, and L. Foster, 372–404. Carleton: Melbourne University Press.

Enloe, Cynthia. 1989. *Bananas, Beaches and Bases: Making Feminist Sense of International Politics.* Berkeley: University of California Press.

Eriksen, Thomas Hylland. 1993. *Ethnicity, and Nationalism: Anthropological Perspectives.* London: Pluto Press.

Feldman-Bianco, Bela. 1992. Multiple Layers of Time and Space: The Construction of Class, Race, Ethnicity, and Nationalism among Portuguese Immigrants. In *Towards a Transnational Perspective on Migration: Race, Class, Ethnicity, and Nationalism Reconsidered*, eds. Nina Glick Schiller, Linda Basch, and Cristina Szanton Blanc. New York: New York Academy of Sciences.

– 1994. The State, Saudade and the Dialectics of Deterritorialization and Re-territorialization. Paper delivered at symposium, 'Transnationalism, Nation State Building and Culture.' Wenner Gren Symposium 117. Mijas, Spain.

Fincher, Ruth, Lois Foster, Wenona Giles, and Valerie Preston. 1994. Gender and Migration Policy. *Immigration and Refugee Policy: Australia and Canada Compared.* Vol. 1. Ed. H. Adelman, A. Borowski, M. Burstein, and L. Foster, 149–86. Carleton: Melbourne University Press.

Fox, Bonnie. 1980. Women's Double Work Day: Twentieth-Century Changes in the Reproduction of Daily Life. In *Hidden in the Household: Women's Domestic Labour under Capitalism*, ed. B. Fox. Toronto: The Women's Press.

Galt, Virginia. 2000. 'Canadians Pursuing Higher Education in Record Numbers.' *Globe and Mail.* Toronto. 22 February 2000. A10.

Gazette, Canada. 1992. Bill C-86. Part I. 23 December 1992.

Gellner, Ernest. 1978. Scale and Nation. In *Scale and Social Organization*, ed. F. Barth, 133–49. Oslo: Scandinavian University Press.

– 1983. *Nations and Nationalism.* Oxford: Blackwell.

Gibson-Graham, J.K. 1997. *The End of Capitalism (As We Knew It): A Feminist Critique of Political Economy.* Oxford: Blackwell.

Giles, Wenona. 1988. Language Rights Are Women's Rights: Discrimination against Immigrant Women in Canadian Language Training Policies. *Resources for Feminist Research – Special Issue: Feminist Perspectives on the Canadian State* 17, 3: 129–32.

- 1992. Gender Inequality and Resistance: The Case of Portuguese Women in London. *Anthropological Quarterly* 65, 2: 67–79.
- 1993. Clean Jobs, Dirty Jobs: Ethnicity, Social Reproduction and Gendered Identity. *Culture* 13, 2: 37–44.
- 1997. Re/membering the Portuguese Household: Culture, Contradictions and Resistance. *Women's Studies International Forum: Special Issue on 'Concepts of Home'* 20, 3: 387–96.
- 1999. Gendered Violence in War: Reflections on Transnationalist and Comparative Frameworks in Militarized Conflict Zones. *Engendering Forced Migration: Theory and Practice*, ed. Doreen Indra, 83–93. New York and Oxford: Berghahn Books.
Giles, Wenona, and Sedef Arat-Koc. 1994. *Maid in the Market: Women's Paid Domestic Labour*. Halifax: Fernwood Publishing.
Giles, Wenona, and Ilda Januário. 1987. The Lone Woman: Migration of Portuguese Single Women to Montreal and London. *Canadian Women's Studies Journal: Special Issue on the Immigration of Mediterranean Women to Canada* 8, 2: 43–6.
Giles, Wenona, and Jennifer Hyndman. Forthcoming. *Sites of Violence: Gender and Conflict Zones*. Berkeley: University of California Press.
Giles, Wenona, and Valerie Preston. 1996. The Domestication of Women's Work: A Comparison of Chinese and Portuguese Immigrant Women Homeworkers. *Studies in Political Economy*, no. 51 (Fall): 147–81.
Gilroy, Paul. 1990. It Ain't Where You're From, It's Where You're At: The Dialectics of Diasporic Identification. *Third Text* (Winter): 3–16.
- 1993. *The Black Atlantic: Modernity and Double Consciousness*. Cambridge, Mass.: Harvard University Press.
Glick Schiller, Nina, Linda Basch, and Cristina Szanton Blanc. 1995. From Immigrant to Transmigrant: Theorizing Transnational Migration. *Anthropological Quarterly* 68, no. 1: 48–63.
Gmelch, George. 1980. Return Migration. *Annual Review of Anthropology* 9: 135–59.
Godinho, Vitorino Magalhães. 1971. *Estrutura da Antiga Sociedade Portuguesa*. Lisbon: Colecção Temas Portuguesos.
Grewal, Inderpal, and Caren Kaplan. 1994. Introduction: Transnational Feminist Practices and Questions of Postmodernity. In *Scattered Hegemonies: Post-Modernity and Transnational Feminist Practices*, ed. I. Grewal and C. Kaplan, 1–33. Minneapolis: University of Minnesota Press.
Grosner, Lucia Beatriz Barros. 1991. *Azorean Portuguese Women in London, Ontario: The Construction of Gender*. M.A. thesis, Department of Anthropology, University of Western Ontario.

Grosner, Lucia. 1995. *A Canadian Profile: Toronto's Portuguese and Brazilian Communities: Information and Resource Guide*. Toronto: Portuguese Interagency Network.

Hall, Stuart. 1991. The Local and the Global: Globalization and Ethnicity. In *Culture, Globalization and the World System*, ed. Anthony King, 19–39. London: Macmillan.

Hamilton, R., and M. Barrett. 1987. *The Politics of Diversity: Feminism, Marxism and Nationalism*. Montreal: Book Centre Inc.

Hannerz, Ulf. 1987. The World in Creolization. In *Africa* 57, no. 4: 546–59.

– 1989. Notes on the Global Ecumene. *Public Culture* 1, no. 2: 67–75.

Harzig, Christiane. 1999. 'The Movement of 100 Girls': 1950s Canadian Immigration Policy and the Market for Domestic Labour. *Zeitschinft fur Kanada-Studien* 36, no. 2: 131–46.

Hawkins, Freda. 1988. *Canada and Immigration: Public Policy and Public Concern*, 2nd ed. Montreal and Kingston: McGill-Queen's University Press.

Higgs, David. 1982. *The Portuguese in Canada*. Toronto: Canadian Historical Association with the support of Multiculturalism Canada.

– 1990. *Portuguese Migration in Global Perspective*. Toronto: The Multicultural History Society of Ontario.

Hobsbawm, E.J. 1990. Nationalism in the Late Twentieth Century. In *Nations and Nationalism since 1780*, 163–83. Cambridge, Mass.: Cambridge University Press.

Hoerder, Dirk. 2000. Immigrant Lives, Societal Structures: Human Agency in Acculturation Processes. *Bulletin of the Royal Insititute for Inter-Faith Studies* 2, no. 1 (Spring): 97–119.

Howard-Hassman, Rhoda E. 1999. 'Canadian' as an Ethnic Category: Implication for Multiculturalism and National Unity. *Canadian Public Policy* 25, no. 4: 523–37.

– 2000. Rebuttal to Abu-Laban and Stasiulis. *Canadian Public Policy* 26, no. 4: 489–93.

Hyndman, Jennifer. 1996. Organizing Women: UN Approaches to Gender and Culture among the Displaced. Paper presented at the Women in Conflict Zones Network Meeting, 16–18 November, York University, Toronto.

– 1999. Gender and Canadian Immigration Policy: A Current Snapshot. *Canadian Women's Studies Journal* 19, no. 3: 6–10.

Iacovetta, Franca. 1992. *Such Hardworking People: Italian Immigrants in Postwar Toronto*. Montreal and Kingston: McGill-Queen's University Press.

Immigration Act. 1976. Ottawa: Queen's Printer for Canada.

Immigration Legislative Review Advisory Group (ILRAG). 1997. *Not Just*

Numbers: A Canadian Framework for Future Immigration. Immigration Legislative Review. Ottawa: Minister of Public Works and Government Services Canada.

Indra, Doreen. 1996. 'Conflict Zone' and 'Citizenship' – Situations of Everyday Gendered Violence and Conflict within Newly Formed States. Paper presented at the Women in Conflict Zones Network Meeting, 16–18 November, York University, Toronto.

Indra, Doreen. 1999. Not a 'Room of One's Own': Engendering Forced Migration Knowledge and Practice. In *Engendering Forced Migration: Theory and Practice*, 1–22. New York and Oxford: Berghahn Books.

Januário, Ilda. 1988. Les activités économiques des femmes immigrantes portugaises au Portugal et à Montréal à travers les récits de vie. M.Sc. Département d' Anthropologie, Université de Montréal.

Januário, Ilda, and Manuela Marujo. 2000. Voices of Portuguese Immigrant Women. In *The Portuguese in Canada: From the Sea to the City*, ed. C. Teixeira and M.P. Da Rosa, 97–111. Toronto: University of Toronto Press.

Jayawardena, Kumari. 1986. *Feminism and Nationalism in the Third World*. London: Zed.

Junta da Emigracão de Portugal. 1966. *Comunidades Portuguesas* 2: 6.

Kearney, Michael. 1991. Borders and Boundaries of State and Self at the End of the Empire. *Journal of Historical Sociology* 4, no. 1: 52–74.

Klausner, D. 1986: Beyond Separate Spheres: Linking Production with Social Reproduction and Consumption. *Environment and Planning D: Society and Space* 4, 29–40.

Labelle, M., G. Turcotte, Kempeneers, M, and D. Meintel. 1987. *Histoires d'Immigrées, Itineraires d'Ouvrières Colombiennes, Grecques, Haïtiennes et Portugaises de Montréal*. Montreal: Boréal.

Laclau, Ernesto. 1977. *Politics and Ideology in Marxist Theory*. London: Verso.

Lamphere, Louise. 1987. *From Working Daughters to Working Mothers: Immigrant Women in a New England Industrial Community*. Ithaca: Cornell University Press.

Leach, Belinda. 1992. *Ideas about Work and Family: Outwork in Contemporary Ontario*. Unpublished Ph.D. thesis, Department of Anthropology, University of Toronto.

Leach, Belinda. 1993. 'Flexible' Work, Precarious Future: Some Lessons from the Canadian Clothing Industry. *Canadian Review of Sociology and Anthropology* 30, no. 1: 64–82.

Li, Peter S. 1988. *Ethnic Inequality in a Class Society*. Toronto: Wall and Thompson.

Lipsig-Mummé, Carla. 1983. The Renaissance of Homeworking in Developed Economies. *Industrial Relations*, no. 38: 545–67.

Livingstone, D.W., and J.M. Mangan. 1996. *Recast Dreams: Class and Gender Consciousness in Steeltown*, 1–21, Toronto: Garamond Press.

Luxton, Meg. 1980: *More Than a Labour of Love: Three Generations of Women's Work in the Home*. Toronto: Women's Press.

Luxton, Meg, and Harriet Rosenberg. 1986. *Through the Kitchen Window: The Politics of Home and Family*. Toronto: Garamond Press.

MacKenzie, Suzanne. 1988. Building Women, Building Cities: Toward Gender Sensitive Theory in the Environmental Disciplines. In *Life Spaces: Gender, Household, Employment*, eds. C. Andrew, and B.M. Milroy, 13–30 Vancouver: University of British Columbia Press.

Malos, Ellen. 1980. *The Politics of Housework*. London: Allison and Busby.

Marques, Domingos and João Medeiros. 1980. *Portuguese Immigrants: 25 Years in Canada*. Toronto: West End YMCA.

Martin, Jeannie. 1984. Non-English Speaking Women: Production and Social Reproduction. In *Ethnicity, Class and Gender in Australia*, ed. Gill Bottomley and Marie M. de Lepervanche, 109–22. Sydney: George Allen and Unwin.

McAll, Chris. 1990. *Class, Ethnicity and Social Inequality*. Kingston and Montreal: McGill-Queen's University.

McClintock, Anne. 1993. Family Feuds: Gender, Nationalism and the Family. *Feminist Review*, no. 44: 62–80.

McClintock, Anne. 1995. *Imperial Leather: Race, Gender and Sexuality in the Colonial Context*. London: Routledge.

Meintel, Deirdre. 1992. Ethnic Fundamentalism as a Model of Social Belonging. Paper presented at the Canadian Anthropology Society Conference, May 1992, Montreal.

– 2000. Identity Issues among Young Adults of Immigrant Background in Montreal. *Horizontes* (Brésil), no. 14: 13–38.

Melo, Pedro Miguel. 1997. *The Life History of Portuguese Return Migrants: A Canadian-Azorean Case Study*. M.A. thesis, Department of Geography, Toronto: York University.

Miles, Robert. 1992. Migration, Racism and the Nation-State in Contemporary Europe. In *Deconstructing a Nation: Immigration, Multiculturalism and Racism in 90s Canada*, ed. V. Satzewich, 21–46. Halifax: Fernwood Publishing.

– 1996. *Racism and Public Policy*. Paper presented at summer session of the Centre for Refugee Studies. York University, Toronto.

Miles, Robert, and Victor Satzewich. 1990. Migration, Racism and 'Postmodern' Capitalism. *Economy and Society* 19, no. 3: 334–58.

Mojab, Shahrzad. 1999. Deskilling Immigrant Women. *Canadian Women's Studies Journal: Special Issue on Immigrant and Refugee Women* 19, no. 3: 123–8.

Morokvasic, Mirjana, ed. 1984. *International Migration Review*. Special Issue on Women and Migration, 18, no. 4: 886–907.

Mouffe, Chantal. 1979. Introduction. *Gramsci and Marxist Theory*, ed. Chantal Mouffe, 1–18. London: Routledge and Kegan Paul.

– 1992. Feminism, Citizenship and Radical Democratic Politics. In *Feminists Theorize the Political*, ed. J. Butler and J. Scott, 369–84. New York: Routledge.

Murdie, Robert. 1994. Economic Restructuring and Social Polarization in Toronto: Impacts on an Immigrant Population. Department of Geography, York University. Mimeo.

Neal, Rusty, and Virginia Neale. 1987. 'As Long as You Know How To Do Housework': Portuguese-Canadian Women and the Office Cleaning Industry in Toronto. *Canadian Women's Studies Journal* 16, no. 1. 39–41.

Neal, Rusty. 1994. Public Homes: Subcontracting and the Experience of Cleaning. In *Maid in the Market: Women's Paid Domestic Labour*, eds. Wenona Giles and Sedef Arat-Koc, 65–79. Halifax: Fernwood Publishing.

Ng, Roxana. 1993. Sexism, Racism and Canadian Nationalism. In *Feminism and the Politics of Difference*, eds. Sneja Gunew and Anna Yeatman, 197–211. Boulder: Westview Press.

Ng, Roxana, and Alma Estable. 1987. Immigrant Women in the Labour Force: An Overview of Present Knowledge and Research Gaps. *Resources for Feminist Research* 16, no. 1. 29–33.

Noivo, Edite. 1992. *Family Life-Worlds and Social Injuries: Three Generations of Portuguese Canadians*. Ph.D. dissertation, Department of Sociology, University of Montreal.

– 1997. *Inside Ethnic Families: Three Generations of Portuguese-Canadians*. Montreal and Kingston: McGill-Queen's University Press.

Nunes, Fernando José Cristóvão. 1998. *Portuguese-Canadians from Sea to Sea: A National Needs Assessment*. Toronto: Portuguese-Canadian National Congress.

– 1999. *Portuguese-Canadians and Academic Underachievement: A Community-Based Participatory Research Project*. Ph.D. thesis, Department of Adult Education, Ontario Institute for Studies in Education, University of Toronto.

OCASI (Ontario Council of Agencies Serving Immigrants). 1998. Response to the Immigration Legislative Review Advisory Group Report 'Not Just Numbers, A Canadian Framework for Future Immigration.' Submission to the Honourable Lucienne Robillard, Minister of Citizenship and Immigration. 4 March 1998. Toronto.

Pateman, Carole. 1989. *The Disorder of Women: Democracy, Feminism and Political Theory*. Stanford, Calif.: Stanford University Press.

Peterson, Spike. 1996. The Politics of Identification in the Context of Globalization. *Women's Studies International Forum* 19, nos. 1/2: 5–15.

Phizacklea, Annie, ed. 1983. *One Way Ticket: Migration and Female Labour*. London: Routledge and Kegan Paul.

Picchio, Antonella. 1992. *Social Reproduction: The Political Economy of the Labour Market*. Cambridge: Cambridge University Press.

Pickvance, C.G. 1976. Housing, Reproduction of Capital, and Reproduction of Labour Power: Some Recent French Work. *Antipode* 8, no. 1: 58–68.

Portes, Alejandro, ed. 1994. *Special Issue of the International Migration Review: The New Second-Generation*, 28, no. 4: 632–9.

Portuguese Interagency Network (PIN). 1982. The Portuguese Community of Toronto: Needs and Services. Conference proceedings, Toronto, May 1982.

Poulantzas, Nicos. 1978. *Classes in Contemporary Capitalism*. London: Verso.

Preston, Valerie, and Wenona Giles. 1997. Ethnicity, Gender and Labour Markets in Canada: A Case Study of Immigrant Women in Toronto. *Canadian Journal of Urban Research* 6, no. 2: 135–56.

Quinn, Naomi. 1986. Panel discussion, 'Speaking Women: Representation of Contemporary American Femininity,' Annual Meetings of the American Anthropological Association, Philadelphia, 5 December. Quoted in M. di Leonardo, *Gender at the Crossroads of Knowledge: Feminist Anthropology in the Postmodern Era* (Berkeley: University of California Press, 1991): 30.

Ram, Kalpana. 1991. Moving in from the Margins: Gender as the Centre of Cultural Contestation of Power Relations in South India. In *Intersexions: Gender/Class/Culture/Ethnicity*, ed. Gill Bottomley, Marie de Lepervanche, and Jeannie Martin, 1–13. Sydney: Allen and Unwin.

Richmond, Anthony. 1990. Education and Qualifications of Caribbean Immigrants and Their Children in Britain and Canada. In *In Search of a Better Life: Perspectives on Migration from the Caribbean*, ed. R.W. Palmer, 73–90. New York: Praeger.

Robbins, Derek. 1991. *The Work of Pierre Bourdieu*. Buckingham: Open University Press.

Rocha-Trindade, Maria Beatriz. 1993. Portugal and Spain: Culture of Migration. In *The Politics of Migration Policies: Settlement and Integration – The First World into the 1990s*, ed. Daniel Kubat, 262–80. New York: Center for Migration Studies.

– 2000. The Portuguese Diaspora. In *The Portuguese in Canada: From the Sea to the City*, eds. C. Teixeira and M.P. Da Rosa, 15–33. Toronto: University of Toronto Press.

Rolo, João. 1998. Conference Report: 'It's Time to Inherit the Future: Portuguese Canadian National Youth Conference,' 23–5 May 1997.

Rowbotham, Sheila. 1973. *Hidden from History: 300 Years of Women's Oppression and the Fight Against It*. Toronto: Pluto Press.

Sales, Rosemary, and Jeanne Gregory. 1996. Gender, Racism and International

Migration in Global European Cities. *Social Politics* 3, nos. 2/3 (Summer/
Fall): 331–50.

Sarup, Madan. 1994. Home and Identity. In *Travellers' Tales: Narratives of Home
and Displacement*, eds. G. Robertson, M. Mash, L. Tickner, J. Bird, B. Curtis,
and T. Putnam, 93–104. London: Routledge.

Sassen, Saskia. 1990. *The Global City*. Princeton: Princeton University. Princeton.

Scott, Joan W. 1988. *Gender and the Politics of History*. New York: Columbia
University Press.

Seager, Joni. 1997. *The State of Women in the World Atlas*. Revised edition.
London: Penguin Books.

Sen, Gita. 1995. Keynote address presented at the NGO Forum on Women,
13 August. Hairou, China.

Seward S., and McDade K. 1988. *Immigrant Women in Canada: A Policy Perspective*. Ottawa: Canadian Advisory Council on the Status of Women.

Smith, Estellie. 1980. The Portuguese Female Immigrant: The 'Marginal Man.'
International Migration Review 14, no. 1: 77–92.

Stasiulis, Daiva. 1987. Rainbow Feminism: Perspectives on Minority Women
in Canada. *Resources for Feminist Research* 16, no. 1: 5–9.

– 1999. Relational Positionalities of Nationalisms, Racisms and Feminisms. In
*Between Woman and Nation: Nationalisms, Transnational Feminisms and the
State*, ed. C. Kaplan, N. Alarcón, and M. Moallem, 182–218. Durham: Duke
University Press.

Stasiulis, Daiva, and Abigail B. Bakan. 1997. Negotiating Citizenship: The
Case of Foreign Domestic Workers in Canada. *Feminist Review*, no. 57:
112–39.

Stasiulis, Daiva, and Radha Jhappan. 1995. The Fractious Politics of a Settler
Society: Canada. In Stasiulis and Yuval Davis (1995), 95–131.

Stasiulis, Daiva, and Nira Yuval-Davis. 1995. Introduction to *Unsettling Settler
Societies: Articulations of Gender, Race, Ethnicity and Class*, 1–38. London: Sage.

Statistics Canada. 1981. Public Use Sample Tapes.

Statistics Canada. 1986. Table 10. Immigrant Population by Selected Places of
Birth, Showing Period of Immigration by Sex, for Census Metropolitan
Areas, 1986 Census – 20% Sample Data, Government of Canada.

Statistics Canada. 1986, 1991, 1996. Public Use Microdata Files.

Statistics Canada. 1991. Table 1 in *Immigrants from Portugal in Canada*. Profiles:
Immigration Research Series. Census of Canada Report. Ottawa: Government of Canada.

Statistics Canada. 1996. *The Daily: 1996 Census: Immigration and Citizenship*.
4 November.

Statistics Canada. 1998. *The Daily: 1996 Census: Immigration and Citizenship*.
14 April.

Teixeira, José Carlos, and Gilles Lavigne. 1992. *The Portuguese in Canada: A Bibliography*. North York, Ont.: Institute for Social Research, York University.

Teixeira, José Carlos. 1995. The Portuguese in Toronto – A Community on the Move. *Portuguese Studies Review* 4, no. 1: 57–75.

Thompson, E.P. 1963. *The Making of the English Working Class*. New York: Vintage.

Toronto Board of Education. 1993. *The 1991 Every Secondary Student Survey, Part III: Program Level and Student Achievement*, 205. Toronto: Research Services, Toronto Board of Education.

Treviranus, Barbara. 1999. E-mail communication.

Trinh T. Minh-ha. 1989. *Woman, Native, Other: Writing Postcoloniality and Feminism*. Bloomington and Indianapolis: Indiana University Press.

– 1994. Other than Myself/My Other Self. *Travellers' Tales: Narratives of Home and Displacement*. London: Routledge. 9–26.

United Nations Statistics Division. 2000. http://www.un.org/Depts/unsd/social/education.htm.

United Nations Statistics Division. 2000. http://www.un.org/Depts/unsd/gender/4-1afr.htm

Vickers, Jill, Pauline Rankin, and Christine Appelle. 1993. *Politics As If Women Mattered: A Political Analysis of the National Action Committee on the Status of Women*. Toronto: University of Toronto Press.

Wekerle, Gerda. 2000. Women's Rights to the City: Gendered Spaces of a Pluralistic Citizenship. In *Democracy, Citizenship and the Global City*, ed. Engin Isin, 203–17. London: Routledge.

Wright, Erik Olin. 1978. *Class, Crisis and the State*. London: New Left Books.

– 1985. *Classes*. London: New Left Books.

Yuval-Davis, Nira. 1991. The Citizenship Debate: Women, the State and Ethnic Processes. In *Feminist Review* 39 (Autumn): 58–68.

– 1992. Fundamentalism, Multiculturalism and Women in Britain. In *Race, Culture and Difference*, eds. J. Donald, and A. Rattansi, 278–92. London: Sage and Open University.

– 1994. Identity Politics and Women's Ethnicity. In *Identity, Politics and Women: Cultural Reassertations and Feminisms in International Perspective*, ed. Valentine Moghadam, 408–24. Boulder: Westview Press.

– 1996. Women, Citizenship and Difference. Background paper for the Conference on Women and Citizenship, University of Greenwich. 16–18 July.

Yuval Davis, Nira, and Floya Anthias. 1989. Introduction. *Woman – Nation – State*, 1–15. London: MacMillan.

Zolberg, Aristide. 1989. The Next Waves: Migration Theory for a Changing World. *International Migration Review* 23, no. 3: 403–30.

Index

Page references for the notes are followed by the note number, and the page number in parentheses locates the note in the text; *t*, *f*, and *m* identify tables, figures, and maps respectively.

123, 126; language, 22, 97; male
farmworkers, 26–7; male
labourers, 20*f*, 125; multiculturalism, 18, 20*f*, 63, 83–4, 97; points
system, 21–2, 27, 30–1, 91;
preferred nationalities, 226; racial
discrimination, 26; sponsorship,
27–8; temporary migrant workers,
126; women, 21, 74, 101, 127–8;
workers, 12–13, 21, 83–4, 112,
124–5
Canadian nationalism: feminism,
129–30; immigration policy, 3,
130; limitations of, 14; multiculturalism, 3, 122–3, 129– 30;
racialized, gendered, and class
policies, 12–13, 64, 91, 121–2,
126–7, 129–30. *See also* Canadian
immigration policy
casa: ideology of, 39. *See also*
households
chain migration, 35, 39
childcare, 69, 74, 78, 109–11
children: Canadian immigration
policy, 21, 132n. 4 (22); first
generation and, 8, 44–6, 49–52*t*,
105
Chinese, 96, 136n. 6 (96)
citizenship: access to, xii, 121–3; as
class, 124–7, 137n. 3 (124);
definition of, 122; Department of
Citizenship and Immigration, 27;
and education, 97; global
inequities, 13, 112, 126–7;
globalization, 123–6; language, 9;
*Not Just Numbers: A Canadian
Framework for Future Immigration,*
122; participation in, 120–2, 126–7;
Portuguese community, 90–1, 93–
4; Portuguese diaspora, 32;

Portuguese women, 9, 13, 79–81,
82, 129–30
class: Canadian nationalism, 13, 64,
91, 121–2, 126–7, 129–30;
definition of, 132–3n. 8 (31); and
ethnicity, 90; first generation
Portuguese women, 15, 73, 79;
identity, 15, 79, 82–4, 124–5;
nationalism, 90, 124, 126;
Portuguese community, 92;
Portuguese immigrant women,
133n. 8 (31); Portuguese youth,
94–5; working, 73, 92, 106, 108,
110
cleaning industry, 37, 46, 48, 75–7,
79–81, 92
colonial wars in Africa, 19
community, definition of, 128
community work, 48
Costa, Ana, 93–4, 135n. 2 (93)
Council for Portuguese
Communities, 32
cultural pluralism, 23

democracy, 9, 93–4; first generation
Portuguese women, 79–81;
Portuguese community, 93–4
Department of Citizenship and
Immigration, 27
Department of Manpower and
Immigration, 27–8
de Pina-Cabral, João, 39, 61
diversity, 90, 110–11

economic and political policies, 22,
126–7
economic restructuring, xiii, 13–14,
23, 90–1, 123
education: drop-out risk, 10, 45–6;
equitable access, 90–3, 97–111,

www.ingramcontent.com/pod-product-compliance
Lightning Source LLC
Chambersburg PA
CBHW032144020426
42334CB00016B/1222